Careers in Focus

Personal Services

Ferguson Publishing Company
Chicago, Illinois

Andrew Morkes, *Managing Editor-Career Publications*
Carol Yehling, *Senior Editor*
Anne Paterson, *Editor*
Nora Walsh, *Assistant Editor*

Library of Congress Cataloging-in-Publication Data

Careers in focus. Personal services.
    p. cm.
Includes index.
  ISBN 0-89434-404-8 (alk. paper)
  1. Service industries--Vocational guidance. [1. Service
industries--Vocational guidance. 2. Vocational guidance.] I. Title:
Personal services.
  HD9980.5 .C37 2001
  331.7'02--dc21
                                                    2001003517

Printed in the United States of America

Cover photo courtesy Michael Keller/The Stock Market

Published and distributed by
Ferguson Publishing Company
200 West Jackson Boulevard, 7th Floor
Chicago, Illinois 60606
800-306-9941
www.fergpubco.com

Y-9

Table of Contents

Introduction

The service industry has made its way into almost every area of personal and business life, including image consulting, time management, productivity analysis, fitness training, and other arenas. Traditionally, the services provided were focused in such areas as marketing, public and media relations, business plan development, finances, productivity, automation, computer programming, and downsizing. Today, services sold have expanded beyond the business realm to include almost every possible aspect of modern life. You can find a consultant who will charge you a fee to help you plan your wedding, design and build your home, coordinate your wardrobe, walk your dog, manage your finances, find an affordable college for your children, and place your parents in the right nursing home.

Some consultants in the service industry work independently out of their own home or office, and some work on a part- or full-time basis for consulting firms. Small, start-up businesses, mid-sized companies, large corporations, and governmental agencies frequently contract with consultants who have a specific area of business expertise. Individuals are increasingly seeking the assistance of consultants to assist them in their personal lives as well. Many consultants enter into short- or long-term contracts for their services, while others charge an hourly rate.

Some of the nontechnical personal services provided include fitness training, pet and home sitting, house cleaning, errand running, home maintenance repairs, and transporting children to activities. Repair services for items such as bicycles, lawn mowers, computers, small appliances, and televisions are also often home-based businesses.

The range of consulting possibilities is as endless as the imagination. People may operate repair, tailoring, tutoring, decorating, and food catering businesses out of their home. They may consult and provide knowledge about home or office organization, perform home safety inspections, give advice on career advancement, or offer any of countless areas of expertise.

Because of the vast array of personal services offered, the structure of the industry varies considerably. There are, however, certain parallels that can be made across these broad areas. Individuals who work in any of the service fields need experience, expertise, self-motivation, and a general knowledge of business to succeed. Consultants usually develop the skills they offer by working within the field—often in a number of different jobs—or using related work experience and translating it into new skills. The skills and the reputation of the consulting service are dependent on the level of competence and expertise that the owner of the business demonstrates.

Consultants should develop a business plan that will help them establish, maintain, and market their businesses. Many times bankers or small business development consultants can help with the plan. If service consultants seek financing from a private or public source to fund their venture, business plans are almost always required.

Consultants must seek out clients or customers. This may be done through advertising, calling potential clients, asking previous or current clients for referrals, or other promotional methods. In personal services, it is essential that workers continually solicit new business while servicing current clients. As their reputation develops, it becomes easier to maintain clients, and, as a result, referrals from satisfied clients increase. It is vital that consultants keep up on news and changes within the field so that the services offered are the most current.

Managing a service-based business has all the same elements as managing a standard business, even if it is only a one-person enterprise. Salary, staff, profits, marketing, communications, and taxes must all be handled professionally. Questions regarding expansion, services offered, and fees must be addressed periodically.

The home-based consultant must have the ability to work independently, possess good time-management skills, and be self-motivated. Usually persons who are self-employed work more than 40 hours a week and rarely have a nine to five job. Often running an independent business or consulting service can be very tiring and time consuming; however, the work can be very rewarding when it succeeds. Some of the drawbacks cited by self-employed individuals include isolation from other workers, uncertain workflow and resulting income, and lack of benefits. Self-employed workers should realize that they will have to pay their own health, life, and disability insurance. Vacation time and sick days are not paid and actually may produce a negative effect on income.

Pay for service providers ranges from minimum wage to a hefty hourly rate or substantial contract pay. Usually the rate depends on the service offered, area of expertise, experience, and reputation. The law of supply and demand can be a factor as well. The best way to determine the going rate for a specific service is to visit with people who either market or hire the service. Professional organizations can usually provide general rate guidelines as well.

The service industry is currently quite strong. There may be future fluctuations in certain areas of consulting and business services, but the overall need for professionals and nonprofessionals that can be hired on a temporary, as-needed basis will continue to exist. According to the U.S. Department of Labor, the service industry (including business, health, professional, and miscellaneous services) is the largest and fastest growing major industry group; 11.8 million new jobs are expected to be added by 2008.

As companies downsize and cut back on costs, they tend to outsource some of their work to consultants and small-business owners. This way, companies can hire the expertise needed, when needed, and avoid committing to any long-term contracts or benefits. Similarly as layoffs occur in certain industries and job security is no longer a sure thing, the prospect of being your own boss and controlling your own fate is becoming more appealing to a growing population. The option of traveling to another room in your home instead of fighting rush-hour traffic appeals to many burned-out professionals. The increased use of computers, faxes, modems, and the Internet has opened up the possibility of working from home to individuals around the world.

The opportunities for professional and nonprofessional services are expected to grow significantly in response to our fast-paced world and the decreased amount of time people have to care for children, cook, run errands, and handle their financial affairs. In addition, people are becoming more willing to pay for these services, either as a necessity or a luxury.

Each article in this book discusses a particular service occupation in detail. The articles in *Careers in Focus: Personal Services* appear in Ferguson's *Encyclopedia of Careers and Vocational Guidance*, but have been updated and revised with the latest information from the U.S. Department of Labor and other sources. The **Overview** section is a brief introductory description of the duties and responsibilities of someone in the career. Oftentimes, a career may have a variety of job titles. When this is the case, alternative career titles are presented in this section. The **History** section describes the history of the particular job as it relates to the overall development of its industry or field. **The Job** describes the primary and secondary duties of the job. **Requirements** discusses high school and postsecondary education and training requirements, any certification or licensing necessary, and any other personal requirements for success in the job. **Exploring** offers suggestions on how to gain some experience in or knowledge of the particular job before making a firm educational and financial commitment. The focus is on what can be done while still in high school (or in the early years of college) to gain a better understanding of the job. The **Employers** section gives an overview of typical places of employment for the job. **Starting Out** discusses the best ways to land that first job, be it through the college placement office, newspaper ads, or personal contact. The **Advancement** section describes what kind of career path to expect from the job and how to get there. **Earnings** lists salary ranges and describes the typical fringe benefits. The **Work Environment** section describes the typical surroundings and conditions of employment—whether indoors or outdoors, noisy or quiet, social or independent, and so on. Also discussed are typical hours worked, any seasonal fluctuations, and the stresses and strains of the job. The **Outlook** section summarizes the job in terms of the general economy and industry projections. For the most part, Outlook information is obtained from the Bureau of Labor Statistics and is supplemented by information taken from professional associations. Job growth terms follow those used in the *Occupational Outlook Handbook:* Growth described as "much faster than the average" means an increase of 36 percent or more. Growth described as "faster than the average" means an increase of 21 to 35 percent. Growth described as "about as fast as the average" means an increase of 10 to 20 percent. Growth described as "little change or more slowly than the average" means an increase of 0 to 9 percent. "Decline" means a decrease of 1 percent or more. Each article ends with **For More Information,** which lists organizations that can provide career information on training, education, internships, scholarships, and job placement.

Bicycle Mechanics

Physics Technical/shop	School Subjects
Following instructions Mechanical/manipulative	Personal Skills
Primarily indoors Primarily one location	Work Environment
High school diploma	Minimum Education Level
$10,400 to $16,640 to $25,220	Salary Range
Voluntary	Certification or Licensing
Faster than the average	Outlook

Overview

Bicycle mechanics use hand and power tools to repair, service, and assemble all types of bicycles. They may do routine maintenance and tune-ups, or completely rebuild damaged or old bicycles. Bike manufacturers, dealers, retail bike and sporting goods stores, and general merchandise stores may employ bicycle mechanics. The increased popularity of bicycles, and the fact that many riders lack the time or desire to learn how to maintain and repair their bikes, makes the employment outlook for bicycle mechanics good. Approximately 11,000 bicycle mechanics work in the United States.

History

Bicycles have been said to be the most efficient means ever devised to turn human energy into propulsion. The first successful bicycle was built in Scotland around 1839. It, like the bicycles built for many years afterward, had a large front wheel that was pedaled and steered, and a smaller wheel in back for balance. In time, advances in design and technology improved the ease with which riders could balance, steer, brake, and get on and off bicycles. The first modern-looking bicycle, with equal-sized front and rear wheels and a loop of chain on a sprocket drive, was built in 1874. By the early 1890s, pneumatic tires and the basic diamond-pattern frame made bicycles stable, efficient, and fairly inexpensive. Bicycle riding became a popular recreation, and, in some countries around the world, a major form of transportation. In the 20th century, bicycle performance was further improved by lightweight frames with new designs and improved gear mechanisms, tires, and other components.

After automobiles became the dominant vehicles on American roads, bicycles were usually considered children's toys in the United States. However, the 1960s and 1970s saw a resurgence in their popularity among adults that has continued to this day. With the increasing costs associated with cars and environmental concerns, more people are using bikes, not only for exercise, racing, or touring, but also for short trips to the store, to visit friends, or to go to work.

The Job

Repairing bicycles takes mechanical skill and careful attention to detail. Many repairs, such as replacing brake cables, are relatively simple, while others can be very complicated. Mechanics use a variety of tools, including wrenches, screwdrivers, drills, vises, and specialized tools to repair and maintain bikes. There are many different brands of bikes, both domestic and foreign, and each has its own unique characteristics and mechanical problems.

Bicycle mechanics work on both new and used bicycles. They may be required to do emergency repairs or routine tune-ups, or they may need to repair and recondition used bikes so they can be sold. Many new bikes come from the manufacturer unassembled, and mechanics working at a bicycle dealership or shop must assemble them and make adjustments so they operate properly. Many department stores and discount houses that sell bikes contract out this type of assembly work to dealerships or bike shops, and it can be very profitable.

Some of the basic repairs that bicycles need can easily be done by the owner, but many cyclists lack the tools, time, or initiative to learn how to service their bikes. They prefer to take most problems to professional bicycle mechanics. One type of repair is fixing a flat tire. Leaks in clincher tires (those with a separate inner tube) can be fixed at home, but many owners choose to take them to a bicycle mechanic. Repairing sew-up tires (which have no inner tube) is a more complicated process that generally requires a mechanic. Mechanics can also build wheels, replace and tighten spokes, and "true," or align the wheels. To build a wheel, the mechanic laces the spokes between the rim and the hub of the wheel and then tightens them individually with a special wrench until the wheel spins without wobbling. A truing machine is used to test the balance of the wheel as it spins.

The gear mechanism on multiple-speed bikes is another common concern for bicycle mechanics. On some bikes, gears are shifted by means of a derailleur, which is located on the back wheel hub or at the bottom bracket assembly where the pedals and chain meet. This derailleur frequently needs adjustment. The mechanic aligns the front and rear gears of the derailleur to reduce wear on both the chain and the gear teeth and adjusts the mechanism to keep constant pressure on the chain. Gear mechanisms vary greatly among different makes of bicycles so mechanics have to keep up with current models and trends.

Bicycle mechanics must be able to spot trouble in a bike and correct problems before they become serious. They may have to straighten a bent frame by using a special vise and a heavy steel rod. They may be asked to adjust or replace the braking mechanism so that the force on the brakes is spread evenly. They may need to take apart, clean, grease, and reassemble the headset, or front hub, and the bottom bracket that houses the axle of the pedal crank.

Mechanics who work in a bike shop sometimes work as salespeople, advising customers on their bike purchases or accessories, including helmets, clothing, mirrors, locks, racks, bags, and more. In some shops, especially those located in resort areas, bike mechanics may also work as bicycle-rental clerks. Where winters are cold and biking is seasonal, bike mechanics may work part of the year on other recreational equipment, such as fitness equipment, snowmobiles, or small engines.

Requirements

High School

Completion of high school or other formal education is not necessarily required for a job as a bicycle mechanic, although employers may prefer applicants who are high school graduates. If you are considering this kind of work, you will benefit from taking vocational-technical or shop classes in high school. Such classes will give you the opportunity to work with your hands, follow blueprints or other directions, and build equipment. Science classes, such as physics, will give you an understanding of the principles at work behind the design of equipment as well as helping you to understand how it functions. Since you will most likely be working in a retail environment, consider taking business, accounting, or computer classes that will give you business skills. Don't forget to take English or communication classes. These classes will help you develop your communication skills, an asset when dealing with customers, as well as your research and reading skills, an asset when your work includes reviewing maintenance and repair documentation for many different types of bikes.

Certification or Licensing

Bicycle maintenance courses are offered at some technical and vocational schools, and there are at least three privately operated training schools for mechanics. Bicycle manufacturers may also offer factory instruction to mechanics employed by the company's authorized dealers. Completion of many of the courses offered earns the mechanic certificates that may help when seeking a job or when seeking a promotion.

Other Requirements

For the most part, bike mechanics learn informally on the job. At least two years of hands-on training and experience is required to become a thoroughly skilled mechanic, but because new makes and models of bikes are constantly being introduced, there are always new things to learn that may require additional training. Many times a bicycle distributor visits bike mechanics at a shop to make sure the mechanic's work is competent before the shop is officially permitted to sell and service a new kind of bike. Because of this steady stream of new information, bicycle mechanics must have a desire to study and add to their knowledge.

Bicycle mechanics also need excellent hand-eye coordination and a certain degree of physical endurance. They may work with small tools to make fine adjustments. Often much of their work is performed while they stand, bend, or kneel. Mechanics must be independent decision makers, able to decide on proper repair strategies, but they should also be able to work comfortably with others. Frequently they will need to interact with customers and other workers.

Exploring

Many people become interested in bicycle repair because they own and maintain their own bikes. Taking general maintenance and tune-up classes that some bike shops offer for bicycle owners is a good way for you to explore your interest in working with bikes. Visit with the bicycle mechanics at these shops and ask them for their insights. How did they start in this line of work? What do they enjoy most about it? What is the most challenging aspect of the job? If a local shop does not offer classes, consider taking courses at a private school such as the United Bicycle Institute or the Barnett Bicycle Institute (contact information is at the end of this article).

Bike shops sometimes hire inexperienced students as assistants to work on a part-time basis or during the summer when their business is most brisk. Such a job is probably the best way to find out about this type of work.

There are various magazines available at larger newsstands, bookstores, or public libraries that are devoted to recreational cycling and serious bicycle racing. These magazines often include the technical aspects of how bicycles are constructed and operated, and they may provide helpful information to anyone interested in bike repair. Bicycle associations can provide additional information regarding classes, industry news, and employment.

Employers

There are approximately 11,000 bicycle mechanics working in the United States, and they are employed nationwide. They may work in local bicycle shops, for large sporting goods stores, or for bicycle manufacturers. Resorts and some retail stores also hire people with these skills. Bicycle mechanics may also be required to repair other types of equipment or serve as sales clerks.

Starting Out

If you are a beginner with no experience, start out by contacting local bike shops or bike manufacturers to find one that is willing to hire trainees. Check the Yellow Pages for a list of bicycle dealers in your area. Bike dealers may also be willing to provide on-the-job training. In addition, the want ads of your local newspaper are a source of information on job openings. Also, try joining a local bicycling club that will allow you to network with other enthusiasts who may know of open positions.

People who have learned bike repair and have accumulated the tools they need may be able to do repair work independently, perhaps using ads and referrals to gradually build a small business.

Advancement

There are few opportunities for advancement for bicycle mechanics unless they combine their interest in bikes with another activity. For example, after a few years on the job, they may be able to start managing the bike shop where they work. Some mechanics move on to jobs with the bicycle department of a large department or sporting goods store and from there move up to department manager or regional sales manager. Another possibility is to become a sales representative for a bicycle manufacturer or distributor.

Some bicycle mechanics want to own and operate their own bike stores. If they gain enough experience and save or borrow enough money to cover start-up costs, they may be able to establish a successful new business. College courses in business, management, and accounting are recommended for aspiring shop owners.

Earnings

Many bicycle mechanics work a standard 40-hour week. In some areas of the country, mechanics may find that their hours increase in the spring, when people bring their bikes out of storage, and decrease when the weather gets colder. Workers in this field are typically paid on an hourly basis.

Trainee mechanics with less than one year's experience may start at $5 to $6 per hour, which translates into $10,400 to $12,480 annually. As they gain more experience and become more valuable to their employers, mechanics may make $8 to $9 hourly, or $16,640 to $18,720 a year. According to the 1998 edition of the *O*Net Dictionary of Occupational Titles*, mechanics who also have sales responsibilities had an annual income of approximately $25,220.

Benefits vary depending on the shop or facility where employed and the number of hours worked. Some jobs may include standard benefits.

Work Environment

Bicycle mechanics do much of their work indoors standing at a workbench. They work constantly with their hands and various tools to perform the prescribed tasks. It is a job that requires attention to detail and, in some cases, the ability to diagnose and troubleshoot problems. Because of the wide variety of bicycles on the market today, mechanics must be familiar with many different types of bicycles, and their problems and repair procedures. Although it is sometimes greasy and dirty work, it is, in general, not very strenuous. Most heavy work, such as painting, brazing, and frame straightening, is done in larger bike shops and specialty shops.

Once the job is mastered, workers may find it somewhat repetitive and not very challenging. It may also be frustrating in cases where bicycles are so old or in such bad shape that they are virtually irreparable. Most often, bicycle mechanics choose this profession because they are cycling enthusiasts themselves. If this is the case, it may be very enjoyable for them to be able to work with bicycles and interact with customers who are fellow cyclists.

Mechanics work by themselves or with a few co workers as they service bikes, but in many shops they also deal with the public, working the register or helping customers select and purchase bicycles and accessories. The atmosphere around a bike shop can be hectic, especially during peak seasons in shops where mechanics must double as clerks. As is true in any retail situation, bicycle mechanics may sometimes have to deal with irate or rude customers.

Outlook

Cycling continues to gain popularity. People are bicycling for fun, fitness, as a means of transportation, and for the thrill of racing. Bikes don't burn gas or pollute the atmosphere, and they are relatively cheap and versatile. With personal fitness and the preservation of the environment as two of the nation's biggest trends and concerns, the long-term bike sales curve is rising. The U.S. Department of Labor predicts employment for bicycle mechanics to grow faster than the average through 2008.

Bicycle repair work is also relatively immune to fluctuations in the economy. In times of economic boom, people buy more new bikes and mechanics are kept busy assembling, selling, and servicing them. During economic recessions, people take their old bikes to mechanics for repair.

For More Information

To read online articles from the magazine, Adventure Cyclist, *contact:*

Adventure Cycling Association
150 East Pine Street
Missoula, MT 59807
Tel: 800-755-2453
Email: info@adventurecycling.org
Web: http://www.adv-cycling.org

For information on courses in bicycle repair and mechanics, contact:

Barnett Bicycle Institute
2755 Ore Mill Drive, Suite 14
Colorado Springs, CO 80904
Tel: 719-632-5173
Web: http://www.bbinstitute.com/

For more information on the industry, contact:

National Bicycle Dealers Association
777 West 19th Street, Suite O
Costa Mesa, CA 92627
Email: info@nbda.com
Web: http://www.nbda.com

For news and information about upcoming races and events , contact:

League of American Bicyclists
1612 K Street, NW, Suite 401
Washington, DC 20006-2082
Tel: 202-822-1333
Email: bikeleague@bikeleague.org
Web: http://www.bikeleague.org

For information on courses in repair and mechanic certification, contact:

United Bicycle Institute
401 Williamson Way
PO Box 128
Ashland, OR 97520
Tel: 541-488-1121
Web: http://www.bikeschool.com/

Caterers

Overview

Caterers plan, coordinate, and supervise food service at parties and at other social functions. Working with their clients, they purchase appropriate supplies, plan menus, supervise food preparation, direct serving of food and refreshments, and ensure the overall smooth functioning of the event. As entrepreneurs, they are also responsible for budgeting, bookkeeping, and other administrative tasks.

History

Catering is part of the food service industry and has been around for as long as there have been restaurants. Once viewed as a service available only to the very wealthy, who used caterers to supplement their own hired staff for grand occasions, catering today is used by many people for many different types of gatherings.

The Job

A caterer is a chef, purchasing agent, personnel director, and accountant. Often a caterer will also play the role of host, allowing clients to enjoy their own party. A caterer's responsibilities vary, depending on the size of the catering firm and the specific needs of individual clients. While preparing quality food is a concern no matter what the size of the party, larger events require far more planning and coordination. For example, a large catering firm may organize and plan a formal event for a thousand people, including planning and preparing a seven-course meal, decorating the hall with flowers and wall hangings, employing 20 or more wait staff to serve food, and arranging the entertainment. The catering firm will also set up the tables and chairs and provide the necessary linen, silverware, and dishes. A catering company may organize 50 or so such events a month or only several a year. A smaller catering organization may concentrate on simpler events, such as preparing food for an informal buffet for 15 people.

Caterers service not only individual clients but also industrial clients. A caterer may supervise a company cafeteria or plan food service for an airline or cruise ship. Such caterers often take over full-time supervision of food operations, including ordering food and other supplies, supervising personnel and food preparation, and overseeing the maintenance of equipment.

Caterers need to be flexible in their approach to food preparation, that is, able to prepare food both on- and off-premises, as required by logistical considerations and the wishes of the client. For example, if the caterer is handling a large banquet in a hotel or other location, he or she will usually prepare the food on-premises, using kitchen and storage facilities as needed. The caterer might also work in a client's kitchen for an event in a private home. In both cases, the caterer must visit the site of the function well before the actual event to determine how and where the food will be prepared. Caterers may also prepare food off-premises, working either in their own kitchens or in a mobile kitchen.

Working with the client is obviously a very important aspect of the caterer's job. Clients always want their affairs to be extra special, and the caterer's ability to present such items as a uniquely shaped wedding cake or to provide beautiful decorations will enhance the ambiance and contribute to customer satisfaction. The caterer and the client work together to establish a budget, develop a menu, and determine the desired atmosphere. Many caterers have their own special recipes, and they are always on the lookout for quality fruits, vegetables, and meats. Caterers should have an eye for detail and be able to make fancy hors d'oeuvres and eye-catching fruit and vegetable displays.

Although caterers can usually prepare a variety of dishes, they may have a specialty, such as Cajun or Italian cuisine. Caterers may also have a special serving style, such as serving food in Renaissance period dress, that sets them apart from other caterers. Developing a reputation by specializing in a certain area is an especially effective marketing technique.

The caterer is a coordinator who works with suppliers, food servers, and the client to ensure that an event comes off as planned. The caterer must be in frequent contact with all parties involved in the affair, making sure, for example, that the food is delivered on time, the flowers are fresh, and the entertainment shows up and performs as promised.

Good management skills are extremely important. The caterer must know how much food and other supplies to order, what equipment will be needed, how many staff to hire, and how to coordinate various activities to ensure a smooth-running event. Purchasing the proper supplies entails knowledge of a variety of food products, their suppliers, and the contacts needed to get the right product at the best possible price.

Caterers working in a large operation may appoint a manager to oversee an event. The manager will take care of the ordering, planning, and supervising responsibilities and may even work with the client.

As entrepreneurs, caterers have many important day-to-day administrative responsibilities, such as overseeing the budgeting and bookkeeping of the operation. They must make sure that the business continues to make a profit while keeping its prices competitive. Additionally, caterers must know how to figure costs and other budgetary considerations, plan inventories, buy food, and ensure compliance with health regulations.

Caterer helpers may prepare and serve hors d'oeuvres and other food and refreshments at social functions under the supervision of the head caterer. They also help arrange tables and decorations and then assist in the cleanup.

Requirements

High School

Does working as a caterer sound interesting to you? If so, you should take home economics or family and consumer science classes in high school. Any class that will teach you about food preparation, presentation, and nutrition will help you. Since caterers run their own businesses you should also take math, accounting and bookkeeping, and business classes to prepare for dealing with budgets, record keeping, and management. Like so many small business owners today, most caterers will use computers for such things as planning schedules, keeping addresses, and updating accounts, so be sure to take computer classes. English classes will help you to hone your communication skills, which will be essential when you deal with customers. Finally, round out your education by taking health and science classes, which will give you an added understanding of nutrition, how the body works, and how contamination occurs.

Postsecondary Training

The best way to enter the catering industry is through formal postsecondary education. One way of obtaining this education is to attend a vocational or community college with an appropriate program. Many of these schools and colleges offer professional training programs in food science, food preparation, and catering. Often these programs will provide opportunities for their students to work in apprentice positions to gain hands-on experience.

As the catering field has grown more competitive, many successful caterers are now choosing to get a college degree in business administration, family and consumer science (home economics), nutrition, or a related field. If you decide to get a four-year college degree, make sure your coursework includes subjects in nutrition, health, and business management, regardless of your major. A number of colleges and universities also offer assistance to their students in finding apprenticeships. The Foundation of the National Association of Catering Executives, the educational affiliate of the National Association of Catering Executives (NACE), provides information on universities and colleges offering programs relevant to those interested in the catering profession.

Certification or Licensing

As a measure of professional status, many caterers become certified through NACE. To qualify for this certification, called the Certified Professional Catering Executive, caterers must meet certain educational and professional requirements as well as pass a written examination. To keep their certification current, caterers must also fulfill requirements such as completing continuing education courses and attending professional conferences.

Most states require caterers to be licensed, and inspectors may make periodic visits to catering operations to ensure that local health and safety regulations are being maintained in food preparation, handling, and storage.

Other Requirements

The professional caterer should have a life-long commitment to learning. Foods go in and out of fashion, new technologies develop, and our understanding of nutrition and health is always growing. The successful caterer will want to keep up with all these new developments in the field. Because caterers run their own businesses, they should be organized, able to work on tight schedules, and conscientious about keeping accurate records. The successful caterer enjoys working with people and also has an artistic eye, with the ability to arrange food and settings in an appealing manner.

Exploring

One relatively simple way for you to begin exploring your interest in catering is to do some cooking at home. Make dinner for your family once a week, try out a new recipe for muffins, or bake cookies for your friends. If people enjoy your creations, you may be able to offer catering services to them when they have parties. If your high school has a club for those interested in home economics, join it. You'll meet other people with similar interests and may find others to cook with. Some organizations, such as 4-H, offer programs about food careers and food. Find out if there is such a group in your area and join it as well. Also, consider volunteering in the kitchen of a local homeless shelter where you can help prepare meals for large numbers of people. Finally, get part-time or summer work at a local restaurant. Even if you end up working at an ice cream parlor when what you really want to do is cater eight-course meals, you'll still gain valuable experience working with food, money, and customers.

Employers

Caterers own their own businesses and are, therefore, self-employed. Caterers, however, do have many different types of clients. Individuals may need catering services for a party or special family celebration. Industrial clients, such as company cafeterias, airlines, country clubs, schools, banquet halls, cruise ships, and hotels, may require catering services on a large scale or at regular intervals.

Starting Out

Some caterers enter the profession as a matter of chance after helping a friend or relative prepare a large banquet or volunteering to coordinate a group function. Most caterers, however, begin their careers after graduating from college with a degree in a program such as home economics or finishing a culinary training program at a vocational school or community college.

Qualified people may begin work as a manager for a large catering firm or as a manager for a hotel or country club or banquet service. An individual will most likely start a catering business only with extensive experience and sufficient finances to purchase equipment and cover other start-up costs.

Advancement

As with most service-oriented businesses, the success of a caterer depends on the quality of work and a good reputation. Well-known caterers can expand their businesses, often growing from a small business to a larger operation. This may mean hiring assistants and buying more equipment in order to be able to serve a larger variety of clientele. Caterers who initially worked out of their own home kitchens may get an office or relocate to another area in order to take advantage of better catering opportunities. Sometimes successful caterers use their skills and reputations to secure full-time positions in large hotels or restaurants as banquet coordinators and planners. Independent caterers may also secure contracts with industrial clients, such as airlines, hospitals, schools, and corporations, to staff their cafeterias or supply food and beverages. They may also be employed by such companies to manage their food operations.

Earnings

Earnings vary widely, depending on the size and location of the catering operation and the skill and motivation of the individual entrepreneur. Many caterers charge according to the number of guests attending a function. In many cases, the larger the event, the larger the profit. Earnings are also influenced by whether a caterer works full time or only part time. Even very successful caterers often work part time, working full time at another job either because they enjoy their other job or to protect themselves against a possible downturn in the economy.

Full-time caterers can earn between $15,000 and $60,000 per year, depending on skill, reputation, and experience. An extremely successful caterer can easily earn more than $75,000 annually. A part-time caterer may earn $7,000 to $15,000 per year, subject to the same variables as the full-time caterer. Because most caterers are self-employed, vacations and other benefits are usually not part of the wage structure.

A caterer who works as a manager for a company cafeteria or other industrial client may earn between $18,000 and $35,000 per year, with vacation, health insurance, and other benefits usually included.

Work Environment

A caterer often works long hours planning and preparing for an event, and the day of the event might easily be a 14-hour workday, from setup to cleanup. Caterers often spend long hours on their feet, and although the work can be physically and mentally demanding, they usually enjoy a great deal of work flexibility. As entrepreneurs, they can usually take time off when necessary. Caterers often work more than 60 hours a week during busy seasons, with most of the work on weekends and evenings, when events tend to be scheduled.

There is a lot of variety in the type of work a caterer does. The caterer must work closely with a variety of clients and be able to adapt to last minute changes. Caterers must be able to plan ahead, work gracefully under pressure, and have the ability to adapt to last minute mishaps. Attention to detail is critical, as is the ability to work long hours under demanding situations. They must be able to direct a large staff of kitchen workers and waitpersons and be able to interact well with clients, guests, and employees.

Outlook

Because of the strong food service industry in the United States, employment opportunities in catering should continue to grow through 2008. Opportunities will be good for firms that handle weddings, bar and bat mitzvahs, business functions, and other events.

Competition is keen as many hotels and restaurants branch out to offer catering services. Like all service industries, catering is sensitive to the economy, and a downturn in the economy may limit catering opportunities. Despite the competition and fluctuating economic conditions, highly skilled and motivated caterers should be in demand throughout the country, especially in and around large metropolitan areas.

For More Information

For information on scholarships, student branches, and industry news, contact:

International Food Service Executives Association
15724 Edgewood Street
Livonia, MI 48154-2312
Tel: 734-542-9412
Email: hq@ifsea.org
Web: http://www.ifsea.org/

For information on certification programs and catering publications, contact:

National Association of Catering Executives
5565 Sterrett Place, Suite 328
Columbia, MD 21044
Tel: 410-997-9055
Web: http://www.nace.net/

For more information on programs and chapters, contact:

National 4-H Council
7100 Connecticut Avenue
Chevy Chase, MD 20815
Tel: 301-961-2800
Web: http://www.fourhcouncil.edu

Chimney Sweeps

Overview

Chimney sweeps, also known as *sweeps* and *chimney technicians,* inspect—or evaluate, as it is known in the industry—chimneys, fireplaces, stoves, and vents according to safety codes. They clean, or sweep, the chimneys and make repairs, which may involve masonry work and relining. They also educate homeowners and building maintenance crews in how to properly care for their stoves and fireplaces, as well as train apprentice chimney sweeps. In the United States and Canada, there are between 6,000 and 6,500 chimney sweeps.

History

The traditional image of the soot-faced chimney sweep in top hat and tails, carrying a long brush, is still very much a part of the chimney sweep industry. Many chimney sweep businesses and organizations use the image in advertising and logos, including the National Chimney Sweep Guild. The sweep of popular imagination originated in the city of pre-industrial London, with its tight rows of brick houses. Before the introduction of central heating, chimney sweeps thrived. The sweep took on an almost mythical quality, leaping from roof to roof, chimney pot to chimney pot. Unfortunately, the industry didn't have the safety codes, equipment, and technology of today, which resulted in health hazards. Cancer and other illnesses particularly effected the small boys and girls who, long before child labor laws, were cruelly sent into the chimneys to do the work a brush couldn't. Today's chimney sweep, however, working under the strict codes of the National Fire Protection Association, is more closely associated with health—their evaluations and repairs save lives and homes from destruction by fire.

Though chimney sweeping has a long tradition, only in the last 30 years has it developed as a modern career choice. The energy crisis of the early 1970s resulted in many homeowners converting from central heat to fireplaces and stoves. The popularity of wood burning stoves has waned somewhat since then because of fears of fire and carbon monoxide poisoning, but the chimney sweep industry is hard at work to educate the public about advances in the technology and equipment that keeps fireplaces and chimneys perfectly safe.

The Job

The Chimney Safety Institute of America estimates that in 1992, a particularly devastating year for house fires, 39,200 residential fires originated in chimneys, fireplaces, and solid fuel appliances. These fires resulted in 290 injuries, 90 deaths, and $206 million in property damage. It's no wonder then, that many chimney sweeps have worked as firefighters. With an understanding of the damage a chimney fire can do to a home, sweeps not only keep chimneys safer, they also serve as advocates for fire prevention.

The National Fire Protection Association recommends that homeowners have their chimneys, fireplaces, and vents evaluated at least once a year. Just as a dentist will send out annual reminder cards, so does John Pilger, the owner and operator of Chief Chimney Services, Inc. Pilger sweeps, restores, relines, and waterproofs the chimneys of Brentwood, New York, and surrounding areas. "The work used to be seasonal," he says, "but more people are recognizing the need for chimney upkeep, so I work year-round."

Sweeps clean flues and remove creosote. Creosote is a residue that develops from wood and smoke and glazes the bricks of the insides of chimneys; sometimes chemicals are required to break down creosote. Sweeps also install stoves and perform a number of different repairs. People contact chimney sweeps with specific problems, such as too much smoking from the fireplace, or rain and snow getting in through the chimney. A sweep will attach a "cap" at the chimney top to prevent moisture, animals, and debris from entering the chimney. Crown repair also may be needed to keep the rain out.

Carbon monoxide poisoning is another concern of homeowners—sweeps reline deteriorating chimneys to keep carbon monoxide from seeping through into the home. With their masonry skills, chimney sweeps perform much brick repair and replacement. But sweeps don't just keep the home fires burning safely; they also attend to the chimneys and stoves of commercial businesses and industrial buildings. Some sweeps even specialize in the maintenance of the large smokestacks of electric and gas companies, which often involves traveling to multiple cities all across the country.

Pilger makes four to seven stops in a work day. He usually makes it to his first customer's house between 8:30 and 9 AM. Once there, he'll spend from one to one-and-a-half hours sweeping the customer's oil or gas chimney, examining and sweeping the fireplace, and checking brickwork inside and out. He also does a video scan of the chimney, using equipment composed of a camera at the end of a pole. Despite such state of the art equipment, Pilger says, "We haven't even touched the future of chimney technology."

The tools of the trade have advanced a great deal since the days of the 18th century when white geese were sent through chimneys; sweeps would determine how much creosote was inside the chimney from how darkly the geese's feathers were soiled. These days, in addition to the brushes, poles, and ladders that have long been necessary for cleaning, sweeps rely on a number of power tools. "From a demolition jackhammer to a cordless drill," Pilger says. He owns special vacuums, hand grinders, and circular saws with diamond-tipped blades. "The blades are expensive and may only last three to four months," Pilger says. But most of the tools, if treated well, can last a long time. He once had two trucks and four employees, but decided he preferred to do the work himself. "It drove me crazy to get complaints," he says. So Pilger and his wife, also a certified chimney sweep, now operate the business entirely themselves.

Some chimney sweeps sell a number of products. They sell wood and gas stoves, cook stoves, and gas barbecues. They sell fireplace inserts, fireplace glass doors, and gas logs. As with any small business, chimney sweeping involves a fair amount of office work. Detailed billing and client records must be kept, and customer phone calls must be answered and returned. Sweeps must also market their services. Many sweeps work to educate their communities on fire safety by distributing brochures and speaking at public events. Pilger is a past president of the New York State Chimney Sweeps Guild, and he sits on the boards of directors of the National Chimney Sweep Guild and the Chimney Safety Institute of America.

Requirements

High School

To understand the damage done to chimneys by smoke, fire, and creosote, take science courses—particularly chemistry classes. In chemistry class, you'll learn more about the chemical reactions from fireplaces, such as carbon monoxide, that can cause illness and death if not contained. You may also be working with some chemicals to break down creosote glaze. With a clear understanding of the chemistry involved, you can easily explain problems to customers and stress the importance of chimney sweeping and repair.

In business courses, you can learn about marketing, budgeting, tax requirements, insurance, and other details of small business management. A computer course will give you some experience with databases, spread sheets, and other programs that assist in record keeping and billing.

Postsecondary Training

The Chimney Safety Institute of America offers a number of workshops and seminars across the country, which introduce new sweeps to the business and provide continuing education to established sweeps. Training in such subjects as safety codes, environmental protection requirements, chimney construction, and technique helps sweeps prepare for the difficult certification exam.

No college degree is required, but community college courses in small business management, or tech school training in brickwork can help you prepare for ownership of your own chimney sweep service. Some experienced sweeps may even take you on as an apprentice; though the opportunity may not pay anything, it will provide you with valuable experience and education, and help you in your pursuit of certification. Many chimney sweeps have worked as firefighters or in other aspects of fire control and prevention. You may consider applying to the state fire academy for their extensive training. With experience in fire fighting, you'll learn to recognize fire hazards, which is important knowledge for sweeps.

Certification or Licensing

Certification isn't required to work as a chimney sweep, but is highly recommended by professionals in the industry. In its education of the public regarding chimney safety, the Chimney Safety Institute of America strongly advises homeowners to use only the services of certified sweeps. An unskilled sweep may be unable to recognize the potential for fire and health hazards in a deteriorating chimney and may even do more damage in the sweeping and repairing process. The certification exam is a difficult, 100-question test and requires complete knowledge of safety codes.

With certification, you can offer your clients additional security, and you can also receive professional referrals. Certification is valid for three years, after which you can re-test or attend approved continuing education programs. Currently, the state of Vermont requires that only certified sweeps work with commercial and apartment buildings. Five other states are planning to follow suit.

Liability insurance is also important for chimney sweeps. Some sweeps have been named in lawsuits following fires in homes they serviced. Even if a sweep alerts a homeowner to potential hazards and the homeowner chooses not to have the work done, the sweep may be held liable if he or she didn't document the warning.

Other Requirements

You should have good technical and mechanical skills as you'll be working with power tools and construction. Patience is important because replacing linings and tiles and removing hard, glazed creosote can be time-consuming and tedious. Communication skills are valuable as you'll need to clearly explain to your clients the repairs needed and how to maintain a safe hearth. "Good customer service is very important," John Pilger emphasizes. His outgoing personality and background in customer relations helps him to attract clients and to keep them. He also once worked as a fire chief, and this background in dealing with fire hazards and educating the public about fire safety has served him well.

Exploring

Contact the National Chimney Sweep Guild for the names of chimney sweeps in your area, and look in the yellow pages of your phone book. A local sweep may allow you to follow him or her around for a day or two. Because of a shortage of chimney sweeps in the country, many sweeps and sweep organizations are anxious to recruit young people into the business. Speak to a guild representative about apprenticeship opportunities, or find one on your own by speaking to the sweeps in your town. The Chimney Safety Institute of America can also direct you to nearby educational seminars and conferences. By attending a conference, you'll get inside information about the business, and also get to talk with experienced chimney sweeps. There are a few publications devoted to chimney sweeping: *Sweeping, The Chimney Sweep News,* and *Chimney Topics.*

Employers

According to the National Chimney Sweep Guild, there are 6,000 to 6,500 chimney sweeps working in the United States and Canada. Ninety-five percent of the chimney sweep services are made up of three or fewer people. Many of them are literally "mom and pop" businesses, with pop tending to the chimney sweeping, and mom managing the office and telephone. Sweeps are in business in every region of the country, but fare the best in larger cities, or areas with an affluent suburban or rural area. Some sweeps work only within a specific area, while others may travel to smaller towns and into the country where no other services may be available.

Starting Out

Having developed experience as a fire chief, John Pilger bought a few chimney service companies and went into business. "The business can be as big or as small as you want it to be," he says. Though Pilger has had a few employees in the past, he prefers to keep all the work for himself and his wife, therefore maintaining a smaller, more manageable business.

The equipment you need, which includes a truck, power tools, and other special equipment as well as protective gear, will be costly at first. You may have to work for a few years with another business, saving up money and building a list of reliable, paying customers. Once you've gained experience with chimney sweeping and have taken certification courses, you may be able to hire on with a large sweep service or to go into business with another sweep. Large businesses that sell and install wood and gas stoves will probably hire assistants, as will masonry businesses. Some of these businesses will advertise jobs in the classifieds, but your best bet would be to contact them directly. Attending seminars and conferences can help you get to know other chimney sweeps, both new and established, who could prove to be valuable contacts.

Advancement

Once sweeps have established their own chimney sweep service, they can advance by making more connections in the community and expanding their client base. If the amount of work warrants it, sweeps may choose to hire assistants and office staff. Those with a successful business can also afford the best equipment and the newest tools. Chimney sweeps can also advance by expanding their services offered. Some sweeps move into other areas of home repair or offer chimney and fireplace products for sale.

Earnings

The National Chimney Sweep Guild says salaries for chimney sweeps are too variable to estimate. Charges for services are also difficult to gauge. Sweeps working in larger cities and affluent neighborhoods can make much more for their services than those working in less populated areas. Sweeps charge anywhere from $50 to $100 for an annual cleaning, and $50 to $100 for a chimney cap. In areas where many people use stoves and fireplaces to heat their homes, such as in the New England states or the Northwest, a sweep may have four or more cleanings scheduled for every workday. In other parts of the country, the work may be seasonal, the bulk of servicing done in the months following the heating season. In addition to service fees, some sweeps also make money from the sales of stoves and fireplace products.

Work Environment

Chimney sweeps work both indoors and out. Some desk work is required to manage scheduling and finances, but sweeps spend most of their time climbing and bending, working in and around the homes of their customers. They climb ladders to the roofs of the homes to sweep and evaluate, and spend some time down at the hearth within the home. This work can be noisy, due to the power tools and vacuums chimney sweeps use, and it can be dirty and messy, as well. Chimney sweeps need to wear protective gear to prevent health problems. They will also carry their equipment from their truck to their home.

Though some established sweeps can afford to set their own schedules, working whatever hours they choose, others must be flexible to best accommodate their customers. A sweep may work an average 40-hour workweek, with a 24-hour phone number for emergency situations. Chimney sweeps do much of their work by themselves, but some sweeps work as members of small teams.

Outlook

The United States is likely to follow the advances made by European countries in environmental testing and protection. The National Chimney Sweep Guild closely follows these advanced practices and actively promotes new standards to the National Fire Protection Association and other agencies. In Germany, for example, homeowners are required by law to keep their chimneys within code. It may not come to that here, with organizations such as the Chimney Safety Institute of America and the Hearth Education Foundation working hard to increase awareness of the many dangers of faulty chimneys.

With more rigid emissions testing expected in the United States, more home and business owners will call upon sweeps for chimney evaluations. Some states are beginning to require that chimney sweeps be certified before working on commercial and apartment buildings. This will result in more sweeps becoming certified and better regulation of the industry. Along with new emissions standards, the industry will also benefit from technology in such areas as gas usage, more efficient appliances, and better water repellants.

For More Information

For career materials and information on certification and training, contact:

Chimney Safety Institute of America
8752 Robbins Road
Indianapolis, IN 46268
Tel: 800-536-0118
Email: CSIA@CSIA.ORG
Web: http://www.csia.org/

To learn about the industry and educational conferences and seminars in your area, contact:

National Chimney Sweep Guild
8752 Robbins Road
Indianapolis, IN 46268
Tel: 317-871-0030
Email: office@ncsg.org
Web: http://www.ncsg.org

For information on fire protection careers, contact:

National Fire Protection Association
1 Batterymarch Park
PO Box 9101
Quincy, MA 02269-9101
Tel: 617-770-3000
Email: public_affairs@nfpa.org
Web: http://www.nfpa.org/

Dry Cleaning and Laundry Workers

Overview

Dry cleaning and laundry workers dry clean, wash, dry, and press clothing, linens, curtains, rugs, and other articles made from natural and synthetic fibers. This work is done for individuals, families, industries, hospitals, hotels, schools, and other institutions. In smaller laundries and dry cleaning plants, one worker may perform several different tasks. In larger plants, however, a worker usually performs only one job in the cleaning process. Some dry cleaning and laundry workers specialize in one or two aspects of the process. Today, the industry has a national sales volume of over $5 billion annually. Over 160,000 people are employed nationwide in this industry.

Dry cleaners and laundries range from small independent businesses that service families and the community to large wholesale and institutional plants. Many institutions such as hospitals, prisons, and hotels have their own laundry facilities on site.

History

In the 19th century, machines were invented to agitate and wring out clothes. With the Industrial Revolution came automatic washing and drying machines. As the number of hospitals, schools, factories, and other businesses increased, the need to have textile items continually cleaned also increased. Institutional laundries sprang up to fulfill these institutions' needs for fresh sheets, towels, uniforms, and other articles.

Also in the late 19th century, the first synthetic fabric, nitrocellulose rayon, was invented. Eventually hundreds of different synthetic fabrics were invented. These new fabrics called for additional cleaning techniques. Items that would lose their shape or color in water needed to be cleaned with chemical solvents. Even some natural fibers were found to last longer and retain their appearance better when cleaned with chemicals. Dry cleaning stores, employing specially trained workers, were thus established. As needs and lifestyles changed, the dry cleaning and laundering industries have had to adapt their services to meet the consumers' demands. In addition, there is an ongoing need to develop, test, and introduce new cleaning chemicals and processes, as well as to invent more efficient machinery.

The Job

Dry cleaning and laundry workers' responsibilities vary depending on the type and size of facility that employs them. Duties can range from store clerk to delivery driver to becoming involved in any or all of the dry cleaning and pressing process. Many times in smaller laundries and dry cleaning plants, workers may be required to perform several different tasks. In larger plants, the worker may have the opportunity to become specialized in certain procedures or duties. In some facilities there may be the possibility to supervise or manage the processes, although many industries require a college degree to advance to this level.

Sales route drivers are often employed to pick up and deliver laundry and dry cleaning to homes and businesses. Some people bring their laundry to the dry cleaning facilities. Here, *sales clerks* take the items from customers, add up the cleaning costs, and fill out cleaning tickets or receipts. Some clerks may be required to use a computer to do these tasks. Clerks also inspect the articles for rips and stains, mark the items to identify the customer to whom they belong, and bundle them for cleaning.

In the cleaning plant, *markers* put tags on articles so they are not lost. Then they send the items to rooms where they are either dry cleaned or laundered. If the articles are to be dry cleaned, *classifiers* sort them according to the treatment they need. If the items are to be laundered, *sorters* may weigh the items and put individual customer's articles into net bags to keep them together.

Laundry and dry cleaning spotters brush stains with chemicals or other cleaners to remove the stains. Plants that clean rugs may employ *rug measurers* to record the size of the rugs so they can be stretched back to their original size after cleaning.

When articles are ready to be cleaned, *laundry laborers and loaders* take the laundry to the washing machines. *Washing machine operators* then wash the articles. When the washing cycle is complete, these operators load the laundry into extractors. Extractors are machines that remove about 50 percent of the water from washed laundry. The damp laundry is then put on a conveyor belt that takes it to dryers, conditioners, and other machines.

Dry cleaners operate the machines that use chemicals to clean the items. *Hand dry cleaners* clean by hand delicate items that need individual attention.

When items are dry or semidry, *pressers* or *finishers* operate machines that use heat or steam to press the items. *Silk finishers* work on delicate items. *Flatwork finishers* feed linens into automatic pressing machines. *Puff ironers* press portions of garments that cannot be ironed with a flat press by pulling them over heated metal forms.

Requirements

High School

In most shops, laundry and dry cleaning workers learn their skills on the job. The only requirement is usually a high school diploma or its equivalent. Computers are being used more and more in this industry, so computer familiarity is a plus. High school courses that might be helpful include chemistry, computers, textiles, machine shop, sewing, and clothing construction.

Other Requirements

Large plants may offer formal and specialized training programs. Spotters may take as long as two years to learn their trade completely because they must learn how different chemicals react with different fabrics and dyes. Finishers and dry cleaners can learn to do their jobs skillfully in under a year.

Another way to learn dry cleaning and laundry skills is through various trade associations that provide newsletters and seminars. The International Fabricare Institute and the Neighborhood Cleaners Association, which operates the New York School of Dry Cleaning, offer many courses and seminars and also publish journals, newsletters, and bulletins to help workers learn new skills and techniques.

Workers need to be in good health since they are on their feet most of the day and may need to lift heavy bundles. They should enjoy working with their hands and machines and should have good eyesight and manual dexterity. They must also be dependable, fast workers who can follow orders and handle repetitive tasks. Workers who meet with customers should be friendly and have good communication skills.

Exploring

To find out more about laundry and dry cleaning work, students may arrange to visit a plant or institution and talk with owners and workers. Students may try obtaining part-time or summer employment in the field to further explore these types of jobs. Libraries are also a good source of information about this industry as is contacting the sources at the end of this article.

Employers

Laundry or dry cleaning positions are available nationwide, in small communities and large cities. Typical employers range from community dry cleaners and laundries to large institutions such as hotels, motels, hospitals, nursing homes, prisons, some government facilities, and commercial industries.

Starting Out

Persons interested in laundry or dry cleaning positions may contact state or local employment offices or read newspaper want ads to find job leads. Checking the Yellow Pages for local dry cleaners or laundries may provide some job contacts. The best way to find work, however, is to apply directly to dry cleaning or laundry plants.

Advancement

Workers in dry cleaning and laundry jobs generally advance by learning their basic assignments and moving to more skilled tasks. Skilled workers may be promoted to line supervisors or department heads, for example. Employers may also send promising employees to programs offered by trade associations to enhance their skills. Advancement in these jobs is generally limited, however.

Motivated workers may become plant managers after several years of experience. Many businesses, though, prefer to hire college graduates with degrees in management for these positions.

Earnings

Entry-level pay for dry cleaning and laundry workers is often not much more than minimum wage. The U.S. Department of Labor reported a median hourly wage of $7.91 for workers in the laundry, cleaning, and garment services industry in 1999. This hourly wage translates into a yearly income of roughly $16,453 for full-time work. Pressers averaged an annual salary of approximately $14,600. Skilled spotters and dry cleaners may earn $18,000 to $31,000 annually. Pressers can often earn between $13,000 and $20,000; managers, $23,000 to $39,000 a year. Laundry and dry-cleaning machine operators and tenders earned a median annual salary of $14,670 in 1998. The highest 10 percent earned more than $20,740 and the lowest 10 percent earned less than $11,600.

Workers receive time-and-a-half for working overtime and may receive slightly higher regular wages for working night shifts. Some plants award bonuses to fast workers, and many sales route drivers earn commissions.

Some employers provide medical insurance, pension plans, vacations, and paid holidays. These workers generally work 35 to 40 hours a week, although the number of hours available may fluctuate with the amount of work.

Work Environment

Dry cleaning plants and laundries are clean, well lighted, and ventilated to remove fumes. The work is hot, however, even with adequate ventilation. Most laundry and dry cleaning workers are on their feet all day. In addition, lifting large bundles of clothing can be hard work.

Workers stand near machines whose noise and heat may be annoying. They may occasionally suffer burns from the hot equipment. Many of the chemical solvents used are toxic and require cautious handling. Other chemicals may cause allergic reactions or irritations of the skin, lungs, or eyes.

Work schedules may vary depending on the facility. Some larger institutions may require shift work.

Outlook

The U.S. Department of Labor predicts employment in this field to grow faster than the average for all fields through 2008. In the next 10 years, however, automation advances will cut the number of unskilled and semi-skilled workers needed, and most openings will be for skilled workers, drivers, and managers. In the dry cleaning industry, many opportunities exist for workers who can perform pressing and spotting procedures. Job prospects look best for workers who are versatile and who have a good knowledge of textiles.

For More Information

For information on careers and schooling in laundry work and dry cleaning, contact:

International Fabricare Institute
12251 Tech Road
Silver Spring, MD 20904
Tel: 800-638-2627
Email: techline@ifi.org
Web: http://www.ifi.org

For information on careers in dry cleaning and education courses available, contact:

Neighborhood Cleaners Association International
252 West 29th Street
New York, NY 10001
Tel: 212-967-3002
Web: http://www.nca-i.com/

For more information on the dry cleaning, laundry, and fabrics industry, check out the following Web site:

Cleaners Online
Web: http://www.cleanersonline.com/

Funeral Home Workers

Overview

The *funeral director*, also called a *mortician* or *undertaker*, handles all the arrangements for burial and funeral services of the deceased, in accordance with family's wishes. This includes the removal of the body to the funeral home, securing information and filing for the death certificate, and organizing the service and burial plans. The director also supervises the personnel who prepare bodies for burial. An *embalmer* uses chemical solutions to disinfect, preserve, and restore the body and employs cosmetic aids to simulate a lifelike appearance. A *mortuary science technician* works under the direction of a funeral director to perform embalming and related funeral service tasks. Most are trainees working to become licensed embalmers and funeral directors.

Funeral home workers are employed throughout the world in small communities as well as large metropolitan areas. Because cultures and religions affect burial customs, funeral home workers must be sensitive and knowledgeable to these differences.

History

Since the beginning of civilization, funeral ceremonies have been held both to honor the dead and to help mourners in their grief. In all cultures, people have dealt with the mystery of death by means of rituals and ceremonies, often burying significant objects with their dead to aid them in their afterlife.

Embalming was practiced by the Egyptians as early as 4000 BC. Bodies were covered with a dry powdered substance, called natron, soaked in a soda solution, rubbed with oil and spices (and sometimes tar and pitch), and finally wrapped in linen. Mummies preserved in this manner have remained intact to this day.

Modern methods of embalming were developed in the 18th century in Europe. Precise anatomical knowledge and the development of standardized chemical preparations and new synthetic materials enable the embalmer to restore the appearance of the deceased to a condition approximating life.

Funerals, like all ceremonies, are intimately related to the society in which they occur. As society has changed, so have funerals. Emphasis in funeral customs in the United States has undergone a shift in recent years from a preoccupation with the dead to a concern for the living. Today, men and women in the funeral service industry are concerned with the emotional and physical well-being of the survivors. This shift in attitude has amounted to an increased need for sensitivity and empathy in funeral home workers.

The Job

Funeral directors are responsible for all the details related to the funeral ceremony and burial. The law determines some of their tasks, such as compliance with sanitation and health-related standards. Other responsibilities are administrative and logistical, such as securing information and filing the death certificate. Finally, custom and practice dictate some tasks.

Directors handle all the paperwork that needs to be filed, such as the death certificate, obituary notices, and may even assist the family to apply for the transfer of insurance policies, pensions, or other funds.

They assist the family of the deceased in the choice of casket, type of funeral service, and preparation of the remains, which may be burial, cremation, or entombment. Part of the director's job is to be a caregiver and, at times, a counselor. They must deal respectfully and sympathetically with families of the deceased, guiding them through decisions they may not be prepared to make and taking great care that their wishes are carried out.

First, the funeral director arranges for the body to be transported to the funeral home. The director then makes complete arrangements for the funeral ceremony, determining first the place and time of the service. If there is to be a religious ceremony, it is the director's responsibility to contact the appropriate clergy. Directors oversee the selection and playing of music, notify pall bearers, and arrange the placement of the casket and floral displays in the viewing parlor or chapel. If a service is held in the funeral home, the director arranges seating for guests. After the service, the director organizes the procession of cars to the cemetery, or wherever arrangements have been made for the disposal of remains. Funeral directors may have to make arrangements for transporting a body to another state for burial.

Most directors are also trained, licensed, and practicing embalmers. Embalming is a required sanitary process done to the body within 24 hours of death to preserve the remains for burial services. If a body is not being autopsied, it is brought to a funeral home where it is washed with a germicidal soap. The body is placed in a comfortable, lifelike position, and an incision is made in a major artery and vein where a tube pumps a preservative and disinfectant solution through the entire circulatory system. Circulation of the chemical solution eventually replaces all blood with the embalming fluid. In addition, embalmers remove all other gases and liquids from the body, replacing it with disinfectant chemicals for preservation.

The preparation of an autopsied body can be much more complex, depending on the condition of the deceased. The embalmer may repair disfigured parts of the body and improve the facial appearance, using wax, cotton, plaster of Paris, and cosmetics. When the embalming process is complete, the body is dressed and put in a casket.

Mortuary science technicians assist directors and embalmers in the funeral home. They are usually involved in a training process that will ultimately lead to a job as a licensed funeral director, embalmer, or both. Technicians may assist in various phases of the embalming process. Since embalming fluids are available in different chemical compositions and color tints, learning the various formulas is one important part of the technician's job. The technician may also be responsible for helping in the application of cosmetics to the body to create a natural, lifelike appearance. It is important that they use the proper products and techniques for applying them, since the result must satisfy and comfort the people who view the body. After the cosmetic application is complete, the technician may assist with the dressing and placement of the body for the funeral service. Finally, the technician may be responsible for cleaning the embalming area and equipment in accordance with required standards of sanitation.

Mortuary science technicians may also perform duties related to the actual funeral service. They may prepare the casket for the service and transport it to the cemetery. They also assist in receiving and ushering mourners to their seats at the service, organizing and managing the funeral procession, or any other tasks that are necessary for the occasion.

Requirements

High School

If you are interested in entering the field of mortuary science, consider taking classes in algebra, chemistry, biology, physics, and any other laboratory courses available. In addition, a psychology class might be helpful since funeral home workers must deal with distraught families and friends of deceased persons.

Postsecondary Training

Almost all states require funeral service practitioners to have completed postsecondary training in mortuary science varying from nine months to four years. Several colleges and universities now offer two- and four-year programs in funeral service. A typical curriculum at a school of mortuary science would include courses in anatomy, embalming practices, funeral customs, psychology, accounting, and public health laws. Laboratory study is essential in many of the courses and can account for up to a quarter of the program.

After completion of at least a two-year program, the graduate can apply to work as a mortuary science technician. Graduates who want to obtain a license in either embalming or funeral directing must work as an apprentice in an established funeral home for one to three years, depending on the state's requirements. Some schools of mortuary science have arrangements with local area funeral homes to provide students with either a work-study program or a period of school-supervised funeral service work (residency or apprenticeship).

Certification or Licensing

All states require embalmers to be licensed, and every state except for Colorado require funeral directors to be licensed. Some states grant a combination single license covering the activity of both the embalmer and funeral director. In order to maintain licensure, a growing number of states require continuing education classes.

After successfully completing their formal education, including apprenticeship, prospective funeral service practitioners must pass a state board examination that usually consists of written and oral tests and demonstration of skills. Those who wish to practice in another state may have to pass that state's examination as well, although some states have reciprocity arrangements to waive this requirement.

Other Requirements

A strong sense of understanding, empathy, and a genuine desire to help people at a time of great stress are essential qualities for anyone wanting to work at a funeral home. Workers must be tactful and discrete in all contacts with the bereaved family and friends. Funeral service workers must always be compassionate and sympathetic, but also remain strong and confident to accomplish the necessary tasks of the job. Funeral home workers must also be good listeners. For example, when details such as cosmetics and clothing are discussed, they must be especially attentive to the client's wishes.

The work sometimes requires physical strength for lifting the deceased or their caskets. Good coordination is also needed to perform the precise procedures used in embalming, restoration, and cosmetology.

Exploring

Ask your high school guidance counselor for information on mortuary science or check out your public and school library for useful books, magazines, and pamphlets. Local funeral homes are the most direct source of information. Arrange a visit with a funeral director and embalming staff to learn about the nature of the work and the importance and intricacies of funeral service. After becoming acquainted with local funeral homes, ask around to see if you can work part-time, either handling clerical or custodial duties. Finally, check out the organizations listed at the end of this article for more career information.

Employers

Funeral directors are usually employed by a funeral home or are in the business themselves. There are about 28,000 funeral directors in the United States, approximately 1 percent of which are self-employed. The majority of embalmers and mortuary science technicians are also employed by funeral homes, though a small amount work for hospitals and medical schools. Employers for these professions are located worldwide.

Starting Out

After attending an accredited school of mortuary science for two to four years, beginning workers start out as a mortuary science technicians, working under the supervision of a licensed director or embalmer.

Most mortuary science schools provide placement assistance for graduates. Additionally, since many schools require internship programs, students are often able to obtain permanent jobs where they have trained.

Advancement

For many years, most funeral homes were family businesses. Younger members of the family or their husbands or wives were expected to move up into managerial positions when the older members retired. This is changing, however, as the majority are entering the field today having no prior background or family connection. Therefore, the potential for advancement into managerial positions is considerably greater than in the past.

The natural progression in the field is from mortuary science technician to fully licensed embalmer, funeral director, or both. With licensing comes more opportunity for advancement. While many people who enter this field aspire to eventually own their own funeral homes, there are other possibilities as well. One advanced specialty, for example, is that of *trade embalmers*, who embalm under contract for funeral homes. Their work typically includes restorative treatment. Also, an increasing number specialize in selling funeral and burial arrangements in advance. Providing the option to make plans ahead of time can give clients peace of mind. Finally, with sufficient financial backing, funeral service practitioners may establish their own businesses or purchase a portion or all of an existing one.

The percentage of mortuary science graduates who pursue advancement outside the funeral home is small. However, opportunities do exist. Funeral supply manufacturers employ licensed funeral service personnel because of their familiarity with the products and their ability to handle technical problems. Workers may be employed in customer relations or product sales.

Earnings

Salaries of funeral home workers vary on experience, services performed, level of formal education, and location. According to the U.S. Department of Labor, the median annual salary for funeral directors was $35,040 in 1998. The lowest 10 percent earned less than $17,040 and the highest 10 percent earned more than $78,550 a year.

According to the Economic Research Institute, the average starting salary for embalmers was $26,980 a year in 1999. After seven years of experience, they earned an average $35,570; after 14 years, $42,070.

According to the American Board of Funeral Service Education, starting salaries for new funeral service licensees often closely approximate those of starting teachers in the same community.

In some metropolitan areas, many funeral home employees are unionized; in these cases, salaries are determined by union contracts and are generally higher.

Benefits may vary depending on the position and the employer.

Work Environment

In firms employing two or more licensees, funeral workers generally have a set schedule of eight-hour days, five or six days a week. However, because services may be needed at any hour of the day or night, shifts are usually arranged so that someone is always available at night and on weekends.

In smaller firms, employees generally work long hours at odd times and often remain on call and within a short distance of the funeral home. Some may work in shifts, such as all days one week and all nights the next. Occasionally, overtime may be necessary.

Employees who transport bodies and accompany the funeral procession to the cemetery are frequently required to lift heavy weights and to be outdoors in inclement weather. Sometimes directors and embalmers must handle the remains of those who have died of contagious diseases, but the risk of infection, given the strict sanitary conditions required in all funeral homes, is minimal.

In this field, much of workers' time is spent trying to help families work through their grief. Because they are exposed daily to such intense emotion, as well as death and sometimes unpleasant or upsetting sights, there is the chance that the work may be depressing or emotionally draining. Employees need to be aware of that possibility, and be able to approach situations philosophically and with a clear head.

Many who enter this field find that their occupation can be very rewarding because the work they do may help the family and friends of the deceased adjust at a time when they are greatly stressed by grief. They help provide an essential social service and one that, when well done, brings comfort and satisfaction.

Outlook

Growth in this field is expected to be about as fast as the average through 2008. The demand for funeral services will rise as the population expands and grows older. In addition, the need to replace those retiring (more directors are 55 or older than in other occupations) or leaving the profession will spur a demand for newly trained workers.

Despite this demand, there are a limited number of employers in any geographical area, and it might be wise for prospective students to check with employers in their area to see what the chances for employment will be. If possible, students should try to arrange post-graduate employment while they are still in school.

Job security in the funeral service industry is relatively unaffected by economic downturns. Despite the flux and movement in the population, funeral homes are a stable institution. The average firm has been in its community for more than 40 years and funeral homes with a history of over 100 years are not uncommon.

For More Information

For information on careers in the funeral service industry and colleges that offer programs in mortuary science, contact the following organizations:

American Board of Funeral Service Education
38 Florida Avenue
Portland, ME 04103
Tel: 207-878-6530
Web: http://www.abfse.org

National Funeral Directors Association
13625 Bishop's Drive
Brookfield, WI 53005
Tel: 800-228-6332
Email: nfda@nfda.org
Web: http://www.nfda.org

Furniture Movers

Mathematics Physical education	School Subjects
Helping/teaching Mechanical/manipulative	Personal Skills
Indoors and outdoors Primarily multiple locations	Work Environment
High school diploma	Minimum Education Level
$12,500 to $18,500 to $38,000	Salary Range
Voluntary	Certification or Licensing
About as fast as the average	Outlook

Overview

Furniture movers pack and load furniture and other household belongings into moving vans, drive the vans to new locations, and unload the contents. Furniture movers often unpack and set up items according to the customer's specifications. Before the move, they may prepare inventories that describe the condition of the items they are transporting, then, after the move check that the items are undamaged.

Movers are often hired to move household and business furniture. Sometimes movers are employed by retail furniture and appliance dealers to deliver items purchased by consumers and businesses.

History

Until recently, most people did not move very often. Once settled, they tended to stay in the same area for much of their lives. A family might move to a different address in the same town, but long-distance moves and multiple moves in a short span of years were unusual. It was around the beginning of the 20th century, when the automobile began its transformation of American life, that families became less stationary. The trend toward more frequent moving continues to this day.

In recent decades especially, shifting factors in local and national economies have created many attractive new jobs across the United States while other jobs have faded in importance and desirability. These new job opportunities, together with inexpensive, easily available transportation, have spurred many people to uproot themselves from their old homes to seek a better life. Individuals and families also make major moves for other reasons, such as to attend a particular school, to live in a more pleasant climate, or to live closer to friends or relatives.

As our society became more mobile, the need arose for professional moving assistance. Few individuals or families have access to a vehicle large enough to transport an entire household. It is the business of the furniture mover to convey across millions of miles each year our beds, carpets, dishes, clothes, and the almost infinite variety of things we need or cherish. Furniture movers let us keep more than we could possibly move ourselves to a new location. For many people, this helps provide comfort and a sense of continuity in the adjustment to different surroundings.

The Job

Furniture movers do more than simply load and unload furniture into and out of a moving van. Much of their job revolves around planning and preparing for the move. Before any furniture is moved, the mover who is in charge (usually the *van driver*) goes through the house to determine the order in which the household goods should be loaded on the truck. Larger, heavier items are usually put in first to utilize space efficiently and avoid the risks associated with heavy things stacked on top of less sturdy ones.

Before they pack items, movers may make an inventory list of everything that is to be moved, noting the condition of each item. In the inventory, they pay special attention to existing damage to furniture and delicate objects in order to avoid disputes later over possible damage during the move. The customer receives a written copy of the inventory.

Drivers supervise the packing and loading of the furniture into the moving van or truck, drive to the specified destination, and supervise the unloading and unpacking, according to the householder's specifications. Drivers need to be skillful operators of large vehicles and be able to maneuver them in tight spots and be able to back up close to loading areas. They are responsible for inspecting their truck before and after trips, preparing regular reports on its condition, and keeping a daily log. They may have to make sure that their vehicles receive routine maintenance services, and they may be required to make mechanical repairs when necessary. Drivers also see that the inventories of the truck contents are completed properly. They may collect payment or obtain a signature from the customer and resolve various difficulties arising from the move.

Van driver helpers assist van drivers in loading and unloading the van. Following instructions from the driver, they wrap fragile items in paper or cardboard and pack them in boxes or barrels. Van driver helpers roll up rugs and remove pictures from walls. They make sure that all containers are labeled and identify the owner and the contents of the container. The labels are useful in organizing the items on the truck during the loading and unloading processes and also help if any items are misplaced. Van driver helpers may use dollies, hoists, and hand trucks when carrying furniture, boxes, and other items to and from the truck. They pad furniture with blankets and secure the items in the truck into a compact load. Using ropes and straps, they carefully fasten the load in place so items do not move around unexpectedly and become damaged during the transportation process. At the destination, the helpers unload and unpack everything, working under the direction of the driver.

Depending on the size of the move, usually three to six furniture movers are involved in the loading and unloading process. Their specific responsibilities can vary with the quantity and type of goods that are being moved and whether it is a local or long-distance move. If the customer is moving only a short distance, usually the same furniture movers load the van, accompany the driver to the destination, and unload the van. On a long-distance move, the van driver and a helper usually drive to the destination and are met there by a local team of movers who help unload and set up the furniture.

Requirements

High School

Although there are no specific educational requirements for work as a mover, most employers prefer high school graduates. Experience in driving a truck and loading and unloading heavy material is an advantage.

Furniture movers need good oral and written communications skills because they must be able to understand and fill out an inventory list and follow detailed instructions. Van drivers are required to keep records of the material they move and the miles they drive, so they must have legible handwriting and basic math skills. Auto mechanics, English, and applied mathematics are high school courses that will provide you with a good background if you plan to work as a furniture mover. Courses in physical education will also help you prepare for the physical side of the job.

Certification or Licensing

While it is not a requirement for employment, many individuals apply to become Certified Professional Movers as a way of demonstrating their professional qualifications in packing and moving services. Certification is awarded to movers who have completed 25 hours of training, and passed certain examinations given by the National Institute of Certified Moving Consultants.

Other Requirements

You must be physically fit in order to move heavy objects. You will need stamina because you may be on your feet lifting and carrying objects for hours at a time or driving for long periods.

To handle moving vans efficiently, you will need to have good coordination and the ability to judge distances accurately. You must also be able to judge the capacity of trucks so that you can avoid overloading them. An appropriate driver's license, usually a commercial driving permit, is required. Independent operators may need to get operating permission from the Interstate Commerce Commission to transport furniture and other goods across state lines.

You must usually be at least 21 years old in order to work on interstate moves. In fact, individual moving firms may require their employees to be over 25 for insurance purposes.

Exploring

Because summer is the prime moving season, it is often possible for inexperienced young people to secure summer jobs as van driver helpers. Part-time work may be available at other times of the year as well. If a helper's job cannot be arranged, a job in the shipping and receiving department of a large store can provide you with firsthand experience of the responsibilities similar to those of furniture movers. Discussing the occupation with people already working in the field can also be very informative.

You can obtain additional information on this career at the library or by contacting the organizations at the end of this article.

Employers

Furniture mover employers may be local, regional, or national moving companies. Some retail furniture and department stores may hire movers to deliver furniture and appliances to purchasers. Movers are sometimes hired on a temporary assignment basis to help move and set up businesses.

Starting Out

People who want to find employment as furniture movers often contact moving companies directly. They may also locate job openings through newspaper classified ads or the local offices of the state employment service. Moving companies usually provide beginning van driver helpers with detailed instructions on packing procedures and filling out inventory lists before they start work.

Advancement

Experienced furniture movers may advance into various related jobs. Van driver helpers may be promoted to van drivers. Movers may also become *dispatchers* who work in the main office of the moving company and stay in constant contact with moving crews out on assignments. Another possibility is becoming an *estimator*. An estimator calculates the cost involved in a proposed move and quotes a price to the prospective customer. Workers who have seniority and proven abilities may be able to move into supervisory positions where they coordinate the activities of drivers and help plan and direct other company operations. Some movers with enough knowledge of the business and sufficient money set aside might go into business for themselves.

Earnings

Most furniture movers are paid on an hourly basis. Their wages depend on which area of the country they live in, the size of the company they work for, and their skills and experience level. Entry-level workers who pack, load, and unload, but do not drive, might expect to earn between $12,500 to $20,000 yearly. An overall average for experienced movers is $18,500, and some might eventually be able to make as much as $35,000 annually.

Drivers earn somewhat more than helpers. They may have an income of around $18,000 to $38,000, depending on their skill and experience. Many van drivers belong to the International Brotherhood of Teamsters, Chauffeurs, Warehousemen and Helpers of America. The wages and benefits for union members are determined by agreements between unions and employers. Most full-time movers receive benefits such as health insurance plans and paid vacation days, although union workers may receive more substantial benefit packages than nonunion workers.

Work Environment

Movers spend a considerable amount of time outdoors, loading and unloading their cargo. They may find themselves moving furniture in extreme heat, below-freezing cold, snow, or rain. The work itself is physical and fairly strenuous, requiring the lifting of heavy and bulky objects, like couches and pianos. Movers have to learn techniques for lifting that minimize the chance of muscle strains and other injuries. Furniture movers may also spend large amounts of time packing and unpacking small fragile items like glassware, which may become tedious.

In much of the country, the summer months are the busiest for furniture movers. Although the standard workweek for full-time employees is about 40 hours, they may work longer during busy times, receiving overtime pay for the extra hours.

Van drivers commonly work at least 50 hours a week, often under tiring and stressful conditions. Federal regulations limit their hours to no more than 60 hours on duty in any seven-day period. Also, after drivers have driven for 10 hours, they must be off duty for at least 8 hours before they can drive again.

Interstate furniture movers, including van drivers, spend a considerable amount of time away from home.

Outlook

People in the United States move on the average of about once every five to seven years. This pattern is likely to continue in the foreseeable future, suggesting that the overall demand for movers is going to stay strong. However, there may be periods when fewer movers are needed. In economic downturns, people may avoid spending money by postponing moves or by doing part or all of the moving chores themselves. Employment opportunities will probably be strongest in large metropolitan areas simply because there are more people in these locations.

For More Information

For information on careers and certification in the moving and storage industry, contact:

American Moving and Storage Association
1611 Duke Street
Alexandria, VA 22314
Tel: 703-683-7410
Email: amconf@amconf.org
Web: http://www.moving.org/

Household Workers

School Subjects
Business
Family and consumer science

Personal Skills
Following instructions
Helping/teaching

Work Environment
Primarily indoors
Primarily one location

Minimum Education Level
High school diploma

Salary Range
$9,790 to $18,240 to $57,600+

Certification or Licensing
Voluntary

Outlook
About as fast as the average

Overview

The category of *household workers* includes a number of occupations, all of which are concerned with the home. Household workers may clean homes, plan and cook meals, do laundry, administer the household account books, and perform numerous other duties, as well as gardening and household maintenance. There are currently more than 900,000 household workers who are responsible for the well-being of private residences and the people who inhabit them.

History

For centuries, the size of a person's household staff was a measure of wealth and status. While this may be true today to some extent, demand for household help has also been spurred by the rise in the general standard of living for most Americans and the increasing role of women in the workforce. Even families of modest means can often afford to hire help for a few hours to assist with cleaning or a caretaker to do household and garden maintenance on occasion. In the past, household work in the United States was often considered the first work-step on the economic ladder for immigrant families. Now the sons and daughters of those immigrant workers run many of the agencies that operate household services businesses.

The Job

The nature of the tasks performed by household workers can best be described by function. The *general houseworker* or *dayworker* is hired by the hour and fulfills numerous duties ranging from cleaning and making beds to buying, cooking, and serving food. The *personal attendant* performs personal services for the employer, such as mending, washing, and pressing garments; helping the employer dress; and keeping private quarters clean and tidy. *Caretakers* and *yard workers* do heavy housework and general home maintenance. They wash windows, wax floors, maintain heating and cooling systems, do odd jobs, and occasionally mow lawns or work in the garden.

Most households in the country can only afford to hire general houseworkers to work part time. These workers dust and polish furniture; sweep, mop, and wax floors; vacuum; and clean ovens, refrigerators, and bathrooms. They also wash dishes, polish silver, and take care of the laundry. Other duties may include looking after a child or an elderly family member, feeding and walking pets, calling and waiting for repair workers, and performing various errands. Houseworkers may have a regular set of duties, or they may be given different responsibilities each time they are engaged.

In larger, wealthier households, *housekeepers* usually have more responsibility and less supervision. At the pinnacle is the *home housekeeper*, who manages a household with a large staff of full-time workers. The home housekeeper directs the staff's activities, orders food and cleaning supplies, keeps a record of household expenses, and may even hire and fire workers.

The *domestic laundry worker, launderer,* or *presser* is usually restricted to the functions of maintaining clothes. The *cook* has broader responsibilities. The cook plans menus or works with the home housekeeper or family to plan special diets, prepares the food, serves meals, and performs such duties as making preserves and fancy pastries.

Child-care workers are responsible for the overall welfare of children in a household. They may waken them in the morning, put them to bed at night, and also bathe, dress, and feed them. They supervise the children's play and in-home educational activities and discipline them, if necessary. They may also take them to the doctor or other appointments.

Nannies usually care for children from birth to their preteen years. In addition to some general housekeeping duties, nannies oversee the children's early health, nutrition, and education, among other tasks.

Governesses assist in the general upbringing of children, from helping them with schoolwork, to teaching them a foreign language or other special skill, to ensuring that they learn proper manners. They may also perform some regular housekeeping duties.

Companions are on more of a par with their employers; indeed, they often are of the same social background. Their prime responsibilities are to act as an aid or friend to a person who is elderly, disabled, convalescent, or merely living alone. Companions may tend to their employer's personal needs, such as bathing, dressing, and dispensing medicine. They may also look after social and business affairs, read to their employers, write letters for them, and perhaps most important, provide them with company.

Although women predominate in private household work, men also work in this field. A *valet* performs personal services for a male employer, such as caring for clothing, mixing and serving drinks, and running errands. The *butler*, like the home housekeeper, may supervise other household workers, assigning and coordinating their work. He also receives and announces guests, answers the telephone, and serves drinks. He may assign these duties to a second butler. A butler who is in charge of a large household staff is often called a *majordomo*.

Requirements

High School

To be hired as a full-time household worker, you should have a high school diploma or its equivalent. Classes you may find beneficial to take include English to increase your communication skills and ability to follow directions and family and consumer science or home economics classes. If you are interested in a certain area of work, take classes that will increase your skills in those areas. For example, someone interested in lawn care and property maintenance might take horticulture or biology classes to learn about plant life and shop classes to learn how to use various tools. Someone interested in child care might take classes concentrating on child development and health. No matter what your area of interest, however, basic math classes will be useful. If your goal is to rise to a position such as home housekeeper or to own a cleaning business, you should also take accounting and business classes to help you prepare for the bookkeeping and other business aspects of the work.

Postsecondary Training

There are a number of schools across the country that offer specific training for positions such as butler, household manager, and nanny. For many jobs you will not need this additional training. However, those wishing to work in households employing a large staff or those wishing to advance their skills to increase employment possibilities may want to consider this option. Although these training programs can be expensive—some cost several thousand dollars—they typically provide job placement services to graduates.

Certification or Licensing

Those who graduate from postsecondary training programs may receive certification from their program. Such certifications include Certified Household Manager and Certified Professional Nanny. Like the training programs themselves, these certifications are voluntary.

Other Requirements

A good personal appearance and demeanor are very important to a person who wishes to do household work. Because of the close contact between household workers and the members of the household, employers generally look for agreeable, discreet, and trustworthy individuals who have a neat, clean appearance and who are in good health. Much of the work done—whether out in the yard or in the house—involves a great deal of physical labor. Activities can include carrying, lifting, climbing, or standing for long periods of time. Anyone wanting to do this work, therefore, should be in good physical condition and have plenty of stamina.

Exploring

Those who enjoy housework and home repairs are likely to be successful household workers. One way to explore your interest in and enjoyment of this work is to get a part-time or summer job in this area. Although you may not immediately find employment in a private household, hotels and resorts frequently have positions available in cleaning, laundry, or even child care. During the summer you may find business mowing people's lawns or caring for homes while owners are away on vacation. Another possibility is to do miscellaneous household and repair work for elderly people in your community who may want help with such tasks. Churches, synagogues, other religious organizations, or local employment offices may provide information on people looking for such help. Housekeeping, laundry, and kitchen opportunities may also be available on a summer or part-time basis at local nursing homes or hospitals. Volunteer opportunities also exist for those interested in being companions to persons needing personal assistance.

Employers

Employers for household services can range from single apartment dwellers to homeowners with or without children to older persons looking for assistance or companionship. Some corporate apartment leasing companies may also hire household workers to clean and maintain their corporate housing units. Hotels, hospitals, and nursing homes also hire household workers for cleaning and repair duties. There are more than 900,000 household workers employed in the United States. Most jobs are found in large cities and wealthy suburbs.

Starting Out

Most household workers find work through word-of-mouth. Friends or relatives may suggest homeowners who are looking for workers, while current and previous employers may often tell their friends about reliable household workers. Information about job opportunities is also available from local private employment agencies and state employment service offices.

Many self-employed household workers find jobs through newspaper ads. A good source for companies that arrange housecleaning services is the Yellow Pages. These companies will usually ask for previous experience and personal references. Direct contact with apartment complexes, hotels, and motels may also be a good way to get started in the household worker profession. In addition, training programs may offer job placement services to graduates of their programs.

Advancement

Advancement other than a wage increase is generally not available within households with only one or two workers. Top positions, such as butlers and housekeepers, usually require some specialized training. In addition, the turnover rate for these jobs is low, as is the number of households that can afford to offer such positions.

To advance, household workers can seek out new employers that pay more or require more skilled services. Workers may also move to similar jobs in hotels, hospitals, and restaurants, where the pay and fringe benefits are usually better and the work may be steadier.

Persons interested in further advancement may want to look into the certification programs available and seek employment with larger hotels, corporate housing, or other firms that hire household workers.

Earnings

The wages earned by household workers vary according to the kind of work performed, the number of hours worked, household and staff size, experience, and local standards of pay. In 1998, earnings varied from around $10 or more an hour in a big city to less than the minimum wage in some rural areas, according to the U.S. Department of Labor. Dayworkers often get carfare and a free meal. Live-in domestics usually earn more than dayworkers and also get free room and board. However, they often work longer hours.

The U.S. Department of Labor reports that the median weekly income for all household workers was $223 in 1998. This weekly income translates into a yearly salary of approximately $10,700. Cooks reported the highest earnings at $380 per week ($18,240 per year). Child-care workers, on the other hand, reported the lowest earnings at $204 per week (approximately

$9,790 per year). The department also noted, however, that some experienced workers employed in large metropolitan areas by wealthy families could have earnings ranging from $800 to $1,200 a week ($38,400 to $57,600 per year). Those with experience and training may earn more than these amounts. According to a 1999 survey conducted by Starkey International Institute for Household Management, graduates of the Starkey training program who worked as household managers at homes ranging in size from 5,000 to 15,000 square feet had annual incomes from $30,000 to $60,000. Those working as managers at the estate level (homes ranging from 15,000 to 50,000 square feet) had annual incomes of $65,000 to $120,000. There are a limited number of employers at this elite level, of course, and such high paying positions are rare.

Most household workers work part-time, or less than 35 hours per week. Because of this, most household workers do not receive fringe benefits, such as health insurance, retirement plans, or paid vacation time.

Work Environment

The work environment for household workers varies according to the duties performed. Some job responsibilities are done indoors and others, such as gardening and household repairs, may have to be performed outdoors.

Almost all household employees spend their working hours at the family residence; however, laundry workers may work in their own homes. Few household workers actually live with their employers for any period of time. Those who do usually enjoy a private room and bath of their own.

Dayworkers often acquire several clients for whom they do cleaning and other chores on a part-time basis at specific intervals. Duties are negotiated with each employer, sometimes on a day-to-day basis. Even though modern washing and cleaning equipment and materials have helped considerably, housework can involve hard, dirty labor, especially for dayworkers who usually are given the heavier tasks to do. Some added demand for dayworkers picks up during the holiday season, but work tends to fall off for them and other household workers during the summer vacation months.

Outlook

For many years, the demand for household help has outpaced the supply of workers willing to take domestic jobs. This imbalance is expected to persist and possibly worsen through 2008, according to the U.S. Department of Labor. Demand for household workers is expected to grow as more women join the labor force and need help running their households. Demand for companions and personal attendants is also expected to rise due to the projected rapid growth of the elderly population. However, worker supply is expected to remain low because the work is physically demanding and usually offers low pay, no fringe benefits, and limited advancement potential. In addition, some people feel that this work carries with it a low social status.

While the field itself is not expected to grow, many jobs will be available for those interested in these occupations.

For More Information

For additional information, contact the following organizations:

American Council of Nanny Schools
Delta College, Room A-67
University Center, MI 48710
Tel: 517-686-9417

Household Management Technologies
6929 North Hayden Road, Suite C4 PMB 450
Scottsdale, AZ 85250
Tel: 602-397-9169
Web: http://www.askmyhm.com

Professional Domestic Services & Institute
5259 Cleveland Avenue
Columbus, OH 43231
Tel: 614-839-4357
Web: http://www.professionaldomestics.com

Starkey International
1350 Logan Street
Denver, CO 80203
Tel: 303-832-5510
Web: http://www.starkeyintl.com

Lawn and Gardening Service Owners

	School Subjects
Agriculture Technical/shop	

	Personal Skills
Following instructions Mechanical/manipulative	

	Work Environment
Primarily outdoors Primarily multiple locations	

	Minimum Education Level
High school diploma	

	Salary Range
$25,000 to $50,000 to $100,000+	

	Certification or Licensing
Voluntary	

	Outlook
About as fast as the average	

Overview

Lawn and gardening service owners maintain the lawns of residential and commercial properties. They cut grass and shrubbery, clean yards, and treat grass with fertilizer and insecticides. They may also landscape, which involves the arrangement of lawns, trees, and bushes. There are over a million people employed in the lawn care industry; almost two out of every ten workers are self-employed.

History

If you've ever visited or seen photographs of the Taj Mahal in India or Versailles in France, then you've seen some elaborate examples of the lawns and gardens of the world. For as long as people have built grand palaces, they have designed lawns and gardens to surround them. Private, irrigated gardens of ancient Egypt and Persia were regarded as paradise with their thick, green vegetation and cool shade. In the 16th century, Italians kept gardens that wound about fountains, columns, and steps. The English developed the "cottage-style" gardens to adhere to the natural surroundings. Early American gardens, such as those surrounding Monticello in Virginia, were inspired by this English style.

The English also inspired the Georgian style of house design in the 18th century that caught on across Europe and America. Rows of houses down city blocks were designed as units, their yards hidden behind the houses and away from the streets. Lawn care as a business blossomed with the growth of population and home ownership between the Civil War and World War I. The sport of golf also became popular among the rich at this time, spurring further development of lawn care products and machinery. Since World War II, many people now hire lawn maintenance professionals to upkeep and improve the look of their personal lawns and gardens.

The Job

Lawn and gardening businesses may choose to offer only a few services, such as lawn mowing and hedge clipping. But some businesses offer a large number of services, from simple cleaning to the actual design of the yard. Some lawn services specialize in organic lawn care. They rely on natural fertilizers and applications to control insects and lawn diseases instead of applying toxic chemicals to treat lawns.

When working for private homeowners, lawn and gardening services do yard work once or twice a week for each client. They arrive at the residence with equipment, such as a push or riding mower, an aerator, and a blower vac. Workers cut the grass and "weed-eat," trimming the weeds at the edges of the houses and fences. They also apply fertilizer and insecticide to the lawn to keep the grass healthy and use an aerator to run over the yard to make holes in the topsoil and allow more airflow.

Lawn and gardening service owners participate in all aspects of the business, including the labor. They plant grass seed in areas where there is little growth, use blowers to blow leaves and other debris from the yard, sidewalks, and driveway. Lawn services are often called in after storms and other natural disasters to clean up and repair lawns.

"There are a lot of little services you can throw in to keep you busy," says Sam Morgan, who has operated a lawn care service in Dallas, Texas, for the last four years. He does general lawn maintenance for residential yards and some rental properties. "Having some rental property can be good," he says.

"It's year-round work. But it can also be dirty work; you have to pick up a lot of trash."

In addition to mowing yards and weed-eating, he assists with planting flower beds, cleaning house gutters, and some light tree work. Tree care involves the pruning and trimming of branches. Lawn and gardening services may need to remove dead, or unwanted trees before planting new ones. They may also offer landscaping services, offering advice on arranging the lawn. Service owners assist in positioning trees, bushes, fountains, flower beds, and lighting. They may also put up wood or metal fencing, and install sprinkler systems.

"I started the business on a shoestring," Morgan says. "But I learned early that you have to have good equipment." He now owns a commercial mower that can handle 200 yards a week.

Lawn and gardening service owners have additional responsibilities than just lawn and garden care. As owners, they are responsible for the business end of the service. In order to stay in business, owners must balance the budget, collect on accounts, repair or replace equipment when necessary, order supplies, and, depending on the size of the business, may hire and manage other employees.

In addition to working on the demanding yard work, Morgan spends much of his time attending to business details, such as keeping tax records, making phone calls, and preparing estimates and bills.

Requirements

High School

Take agriculture, shop, and other courses that will help you gain familiarity with the machinery, fertilizers, and chemicals used in lawn maintenance. Agriculture courses will also teach you about different grasses and plants, and how to care for them. Joining associations such as the National FFA Organization (formerly the Future Farmers of America) and 4-H can give you additional experience with horticulture. Business and accounting courses are also useful to learn about record keeping, budgeting, and finances.

Postsecondary Training

After high school, you can learn about lawn maintenance on the job, either by assisting someone with an established lawn care business, or by taking on a few residential customers yourself. Though a college degree is not necessary, lawn and gardening service owners benefit from advanced courses such as small business management and finance to help run their business.

Certification or Licensing

Most states require lawn care professionals who apply pesticides to be licensed. This usually involves passing a written examination on the safe use and disposal of toxic chemicals

Certification is not required, but many lawn and garden service owners choose to become a Certified Turfgrass Professional or Certified Ornamental Landscape Professional to gain credibility and, in turn, obtain more clients. Both designations are awarded after successful completion of a home-study course run by the Professional Lawn Care Association of America.

Other Requirements

As entrepreneurs, lawn and gardening service owners need to have people skills and be self-motivated to successfully promote their own business and attract clients.

"I'm a good salesman," Sam Morgan says. He also emphasizes the need to be committed to doing a quality job for every customer. Service owners should have an eye for detail to notice all the areas where lawns need work. They must also be in fairly good health to withstand the hard labor that the job calls for, often during the heat of the summer.

Exploring

If you've made some extra money mowing lawns for your neighbors, then you're already familiar with many of the aspects of a lawn care service. Walking behind a power mower during the hottest days of the year may make you miserable, but early experience in keeping your next-door neighbor's lawn looking nice is a great opportunity for self-employment. Other sources for potential clients are private homeowners, apartment complex communities, golf courses, and parks. Look into volunteer and part-time work with botanical gardens, greenhouses, and park and recreation crews.

Opportunities to learn how to care for a lawn and garden are no further than your own backyard. Experiment with planting and maintaining different varieties of flowers, shrubs, or trees. Chances are, you'll gain valuable experience and your parents will thank you!

In addition to getting dirt under your fingernails, you can also explore the lawn and garden services by reading magazines and books on lawn and garden care. Cable television stations, such as Home and Garden Television (HGTV), feature programming about gardening.

Every summer, many high school students find reliable work mowing lawns. But many of these students tire of the work early in the summer. Be persistent in seeking out work all summer long. You should also be committed to doing good work; you'll have stiff competition from professional lawn care businesses that offer more services, own commercial machinery, and have extensive knowledge of fertilizers and pesticides. Some lawn care companies also hire students for summer work.

Employers

Lawn and gardening service owners work primarily for private homeowners, though they may also contract work with commercial properties. Condos, hotels, apartment complexes, golf courses, sports fields, and parks all require regular lawn service.

Owners who choose to build their own business face challenges such as covering the costs of start up and establishing a client base. To defray these costs and risks, many choose to purchase and operate an existing business. There are a number of franchise opportunities in lawn care that, for a fee, will assist you in promoting your business and building a clientele. Emerald Green Lawn Care, Liqui-Green Lawn Care, and Lawn Doctor are just a few. NaturaLawn of America is a franchise of organic-based lawn care.

Starting Out

Most lawn and gardening service owners start out working for established services and work their way into positions of management or higher responsibility. A typical entry-level job is that of the landscape service technician.

After a few years on the job, promising technicians may be promoted to supervisor positions such as regional or branch managers. According to the Professional Lawn Care Association of America, "once a supervisory position is reached, leadership is the key to success." Workers who are organized, show strong leadership, and can make decisions quickly and wisely will have the best chances for promotion and may choose to start up their own business.

However, not all service owners follow this route. Sam Morgan's lawn service was not his first venture into entrepreneurship; he had once owned a number of dry cleaners. After selling the dry cleaners, he went to work for a chemical company. When the company downsized, Morgan was faced with finding a new job. He decided to turn to lawn care.

"I just went to Sears and bought a mower," he says. Since then, he's been able to invest in commercial machinery that can better handle the demands of the work, and he's found a number of ways to increase business. "I bill once a month," he says. "I get more business that way." He's also expanding his service to include some light landscaping, such as shrub work and planting small trees.

Depending on the business, start-up costs can vary. To purchase commercial quality equipment, initial investment can be between $3,000 and $4,000. To buy into a franchise, however, will cost thousands of dollars more.

Advancement

Once lawn and gardening service owners establish their own businesses, advancement can come in the form of expanded services. Some lawn professionals offer equipment and supply sales. With extended services, owners can reach out to a larger body of clients, securing larger contracts with golf courses, cities and local communities, and sports teams.

Sam Morgan currently has one employee, but he hopes for his business to grow more, allowing him to hire others. "I don't want to be doing so much of the physical work," he says.

With additional education, owners can also advance into other areas of lawn care and become contractors or landscape architects.

Earnings

Earnings in lawn care depend on a number of factors, such as geographic location, the size of the business, and the level of experience. Lawn care services generally make more money in areas of the country that have mild winters, offering more months of lawn growth and, as a result, requiring more care. The size of the client base also greatly affects earnings. A lawn care professional with a small clientele may make less than $20,000 a year, while the owner of a franchise lawn care company with a number of contracts and a large staff can make over $100,000.

According to 1998 data from the U.S. Department of Labor, lawn service laborers make an average of $8.24 an hour, while managers earn an average of $12.22 an hour. The Professional Lawn Care Association of America offers the following summary of earnings potential for management positions: first-level supervisors, $30,000-$35,000; branch managers, $40,000-$50,000; regional managers, $60,000; and successful owners, $100,000 or more.

Work Environment

To many, working on a lawn or garden is relaxing and the opportunity to work outdoors during pleasant days of spring and summer is enjoyable. However, the work can also be exhausting and strenuous. Lawn and gardening service owners fully involved in the labor of the business may have to lift heavy equipment from trucks, climb trees, and do a lot of walking, kneeling, and bending on the job. Depending on the nature of the business, service owners may have to exercise caution when handling harmful chemicals used in pesticides. In addition, they have to deal with a loud work environment because machinery such as lawn mowers, weed eaters, and blow vacs can be very noisy.

One benefit of owning a business is the ability to create a flexible work schedule. "Most likely," Sam Morgan says, "during the spring and summer, you can make plenty of money. There's plenty of work to be done." But some of that work may be in the hottest days of the summer, or on rainy days. With your own service, you can arrange to work regular weekday hours, or you can schedule weekends.

Outlook

The benefits of a nice lawn aren't just aesthetic; a well-kept lawn can increase property value, provide a safe place for children to play, and improve the environment. According to a Gallup survey, more than 21 million U.S. households spent $16.8 billion on professional lawn services in 1999. This is a $2.2 billion increase from the previous year in the total spent on services.

This increase in spending promises a good future for lawn care services. The sale of lawn care products is expected to grow as more houses are built and more people recognize the importance of quality lawn care. The Environmental Protection Agency promotes the environmental benefits of a healthy lawn, emphasizing that healthy grass is not only attractive, but controls dust and pollens, provides oxygen, and improves the quality of groundwater. More people now recognize that a nice lawn can increase home value by as much as 15 percent, according to studies.

Technological developments will also aid the industry. With better, more economical equipment, lawn care professionals can do more specialized work in less time, allowing them to keep their service fees low.

For More Information

To further explore the agriculture industry and for information on student chapters, contact:

National FFA Organization
PO Box 68960
6060 FFA Drive
Indianapolis, IN 46268-0960
Tel: 317-802-6060
Web: http://www.ffa.org

To learn about certification, training, and facts about the lawn care industry, contact:

Professional Lawn Care Association of America
1000 Johnson Ferry Road, NE, Suite C-135
Marietta, GA 30068-2112
Tel: 800-458-3466
Web: http://www.plcaa.org

Locksmiths

	School Subjects
Mathematics Technical/shop	
	Personal Skills
Mechanical/manipulative Technical/scientific	
	Work Environment
Indoors and outdoors Primarily multiple locations	
	Minimum Education Level
High school diploma	
	Salary Range
$10,400 to $24,890 to $39,370+	
	Certification or Licensing
Required by certain states	
	Outlook
About as fast as the average	

Overview

Locksmiths, or *lock experts,* are responsible for all aspects of installing and servicing locking devices, such as door and window locks for buildings, door and ignition locks for automobiles, locks on such objects as combination safes and desks, and electronic access control devices. Locksmiths are often considered to be artisans or craftspeople who combine ingenuity with mechanical aptitude. There are approximately 27,000 locksmiths employed in the United States.

History

Guarding and protecting families and possessions is an ancient practice that has led throughout the centuries to widespread use of various types of locking devices. Locks have been, and still are, used to secure residences, commercial buildings, and other items, such as automobiles and safe deposit boxes. The oldest known lock and key device, which dates to about four thousand years ago and is quite large, was found in the ruins of the

Khorsabad palace near the biblical city of Nineveh. That lock was of the wooden pin-tumbler type, a form that was widely used in Egypt and also found in Japan, Norway, and the Faeroe Islands (and is still being used in parts of the Near East today). The modern Yale cylinder lock is actually based on this Egyptian pin-tumbler mechanism.

Roman locksmiths introduced metal locks (made primarily of iron and bronze), padlocks, and warded locks, which are made with varied projections around the keyhole. They also designed keys fashioned as rings so they could be carried easily, supposedly because togas had no pockets. Another important Roman contribution was the craft of making small locks to be used with tiny keys. Elaborate and intricate decorative surface designs introduced by craftspeople in Germany and France during the Middle Ages transformed locks into works of art; however, these locks showed little improvement in safety and security.

Special machines allow locksmiths to create and duplicate keys for any lock. The history of the industry includes a list of locksmiths who contributed to design developments. In 1778, the Englishman Robert Barron patented a lever lock with double-acting tumblers. Just 40 years later, his fellow countryman, Jeremiah Chubb, improved on the reliability of the lever lock by incorporating a detector in its mechanism. Meanwhile, in 1784, Joseph Bramah, also from England, had introduced his innovative Bramah lock and key, which was to remain "unpickable" for more than 50 years. In 1851, Robert Newell of New York exhibited his Parautoptic lock, which reputedly remains unpicked to this day.

In 1848, Linus Yale, of the United States, patented a pin-tumbler lock, from which his son, Linus, Jr., devised the Yale cylinder lock during the 1860s. James Sargent of Rochester, New York, adapted an earlier Scots patent in 1873 for a lock that incorporated a clock, allowing vaults and safes to be opened only at preset times. Other lock experts experimented with the letter-lock until the keyless combination device was perfected.

Since the 1800s, many other types of locks have been devised for specific purposes. However, the most reputable and the most commonly used of today's nonelectronic locks are direct descendants of the original Yale cylinder, the Bramah, and combination devices.

The advent of new technology in the middle to late twentieth century has led to increased and widespread use of electronic-access control devices. Such security equipment is based on fundamental electronic wiring and utilizes any of a variety of mechanisms, such as plastic credit card-shaped "keys" with magnetic code strips or electronic button-coded doorknobs. Electronic access control devices have replaced manually operated locks in many circumstances, from large building complexes to automobile doors. New lock technology has resulted from the demands by security-conscious citizenry for complicated, sophisticated locks. Because such devices require skilled and knowledgeable care, some say that locksmiths have never had it so good.

The Job

The aspects of the locksmith profession differ, depending on whether one works for one's own business, in a shop for a master locksmith, or as an in-house lock expert for a large establishment, such as an apartment complex or a high-rise office building. However, the essential nature of the work for all locksmiths can be described in general terms. Basically, they sell, service, and install locks, spending part of their working time in locksmith shops and part of it at the sites they are servicing. Locksmiths install locks in homes, offices, factories, and many other types of establishments. In addition to maintaining the working mechanics of lock devices, locksmiths usually perform functions that include metalworking, carpentry, and electronics.

The basic equipment used by the locksmith includes a workbench, various tools, a key machine and supplies. Tools may include broken key extractors, drills, files, key blanks, springs, C-clamps, circular hole cutters, hammers, and screwdrivers.

While at the shop, locksmiths work on such portable items as padlocks and luggage locks, as well as on an endless number of keys. When they need to do work at a customer's site, they usually drive to the site in a work van that carries an assortment of the locksmith's most common equipment and supplies. When on site, they perform whatever function is needed for each specific job, be it opening locks whose keys have been lost, preparing master-key systems for such places as hotels and apartment complexes, removing old locks and installing modern devices, or rewiring electronic access control devices. Because locks are commonly found on doors and other building structures, lock experts often put their carpentry skills to use when doors have to be fitted for locks. And because locking devices are increasingly made with electronic parts, locksmiths must use their knowledge and skill to work with electronic door openers, electromagnetic locks, and electrical keyless locks.

Lock experts may spend part of their working day providing service to those who have locked themselves out of their houses, places of work, or vehicles. When keys are locked inside, locksmiths must pick the lock. If keys are lost, new ones often must be made. Locksmiths often repair locks by taking them apart to examine, clean, file, and adjust the cylinders and tumblers. Combination locks present a special task for locksmiths; they must be able to open a safe, for example, if its combination lock does not work smoothly.

Manipulating combination locks requires expert, precise skills that are honed by much practice. The technique requires that the locksmith listen for vibrations and for the interior mechanism to indicate a change in direction while the dial is carefully rotated; this is repeated until the mechanism has been accurately turned. If it isn't possible to open the lock through these methods, the device may be drilled.

Locksmiths work in any community large enough to need their services, but most jobs are available in large metropolitan areas. Some locksmiths work in shops for other professionals, and others work for large hardware or department stores. Also, many open their own businesses. Independent locksmiths must perform all the tasks needed to run any type of business, such as keeping books and tax records, preparing statements, ordering merchandise, and advertising. A locksmith's clients may include individual home or automobile owners as well as large organizations such as hospitals, housing developments, military bases, and federal agencies. Industrial complexes and huge factories may employ locksmiths to install and maintain complete security systems, and other establishments, such as school systems and hotels, employ locksmiths to regularly install or change locks. Many locksmiths are getting more involved in the security aspect of the profession and may be required to analyze security needs and propose, monitor, and maintain security systems for businesses and residences.

Requirements

High School

No special educational requirements are needed to become a locksmith. Most employers prefer applicants who have graduated from high school. Helpful school classes include metal shop, mathematics, mechanical drawing, computers, and electronics, if available.

Postsecondary Training

There are locksmiths who have learned their skills from professionals in the business, but many workers learn the trade by either attending a community college or trade school or completing an accredited correspondence course. A number of trade schools in the United States follow a curriculum based on all practical aspects of the locksmith trade. They teach the correct application of the current range of security devices, including the theory and practice of electronic access control, as well as the servicing and repairing of mortise, cylindrical, and bit-key locks. Students learn to recognize keys by their manufacturer and practice cutting keys by hand as well as by machine. Some courses allow students to set up a sample master-key system for clients such as a business or apartment complex. In addition to these fundamentals, pupils also learn to use carpentry tools and jigs to install common locking devices. Finally, they learn about automobile lock systems (how to enter locked automobiles in emergencies and how to remove, service, and repair ignition locks) and combination locks (how to service interchangeable core cylinders and manipulate combinations). The objective of such training is to teach the prospective locksmith all basic responsibilities. After completing a training course, the graduate should be able to meet customer demand and standards of the trade with minimum supervision.

Many persons interested in a locksmith career learn the trade by taking correspondence courses, which include instructions, assignments, tools, and model locks and keys. Lessons may be supplemented with supervised on-the-job training with a consenting master locksmith.

Certification or Licensing

Many cities and states require that locksmiths be licensed and bonded. In some areas, locksmiths may have to be fingerprinted and pay a fee to be licensed.

Area and state locksmith associations may require that their members be certified. The Associated Locksmiths of America offers the following certification designations: Registered Locksmith, Certified Registered Locksmith, Certified Professional Locksmith, and the highest level, Certified Master Locksmith.

Other Requirements

Locksmiths must be able to plan and schedule jobs and to use the right tools, techniques, and materials for each. Good vision and hearing are necessary for working with combination locks, and eye-hand coordination is essential when working with tiny locks and their intricate interiors. A good locksmith should have both a delicate touch and an understanding of the nature of mechanical devices.

Each lost key, broken lock, and security problem will present a unique challenge that the locksmith must be prepared to remedy on the spot. Locksmiths, therefore, must be able to think well on their feet. Locksmiths also have a responsibility to be reliable, accurate, and, most important, honest, since their work involves the security of persons and valuables. Customers must be able to count on their skill, dependability, and integrity. In addition, locksmiths must be aware of laws that apply to elements of their jobs, such as restrictions on duplicating master keys, making safe deposit box keys, and opening automobiles whose keys are not available. It is suggested that the locksmith-to-be consult with a lawyer to discuss the legal responsibilities of the trade.

Exploring

High school machine shop classes will provide you with a degree of experience in using a variety of hand tools, some of which may be used in the trade. If you are interested in learning specifically about types of locks and how to work with them, read *The Complete Book of Locks & Locksmithing* (Bill Phillips, McGraw-Hill, 2001) or other books about the trade that may be available at local libraries or bookstores.

It is a good idea to contact organizations that are involved with the locksmithing trade. You might request information from the Associated Locksmiths of America, whose objective is to educate and provide current information to those involved in the physical security industry. Another method of finding out more about the career is to talk with someone already employed as a locksmith.

Employers

The largest demand for locksmiths is in larger metropolitan areas. Many locksmiths are hired by locksmith shops or large hardware or department stores. Numerous large factories, resorts, hotels and industrial facilities hire locksmiths to install and change their locks and to maintain their security systems. Many locksmiths open their own businesses and provide services to home or automobile owners, as well as to hospitals, hotels, motels, businesses, government facilities, and housing developments.

The increased use of security systems in businesses and residences offers many additional employment options for locksmiths. These jobs may require additional training and skills, however.

Starting Out

Since locksmithing is a vocation that requires skill and experience, it is unlikely that the untrained job seeker will be able to begin immediately in the capacity of locksmith. Beginners might consider contacting local shops to inquire about apprenticeships. In some cases, skilled locksmiths may be willing to teach their trade to a promising worker in exchange for low-cost labor. Another method is to check with state employment offices for business and industry listings of job openings for locksmiths. Some locksmith trade organizations may post job openings or apprenticeships.

Students enrolled in a trade school can obtain career counseling and job placement assistance. Trade school graduates should be qualified to begin work in established locksmith shops doing basic work both in the shop and on the road; others become in-house locksmiths for businesses and other establishments.

Advancement

Most locksmiths regard their work as a lifetime profession. They stay abreast of new developments in the field so that they can increase both their skills and earnings. As they gain experience, industrial locksmiths may advance from apprentices to journeymen to master locksmiths, to any of several kinds of supervisory or managerial positions.

After having worked in the field for a number of years, many lock experts decide to establish their own shops and businesses. In so doing, they tend to build working relationships with a list of clients and, in effect, can grow their business at their own flexible rate. Self-employed locksmiths are responsible for all the tasks that are required to run a business, such as planning, organizing, bookkeeping, and marketing.

Another advancement opportunity lies in becoming a specialist in any of a number of niches. Some locksmiths work exclusively with combination locks, for example, or become experts with automobile devices. One of the most promising recent specialty growth areas is that of electronic security.

Such safety devices and systems are becoming standard equipment for large establishments such as banks, hotels, and many industries, as well as residences and autos, and their popularity is creating a need for skilled locksmiths to install and service them.

Earnings

Locksmithing can be a lucrative occupation, depending upon the geographic region of the country and the type of work done. Geographically, wages for locksmiths tend to follow the pattern of general earnings; that is, workers on the East Coast tend to earn the most and those in the South and Southwest the least.

Entry-level locksmiths with no experience generally start out with wages between $5 and $7 an hour, although in some areas wages may be higher. Experienced locksmiths earned an average of $24,890 annually in 1998, while the highest ten percent averaged $39,370. Locksmiths who specialize in high-security electronic systems may earn much more than that. Full-time employees can usually expect general fringe benefits.

Self-employed locksmiths may be small business operators who earn less than some salaried employees, or they may head larger operations and earn more than the average through contracts with numerous clients.

Work Environment

Locksmiths who are self-employed often work up to 60 hours per week; apprentices and locksmiths working in industries and institutions, however, usually work standard 40-hour workweeks. Some locksmith businesses may offer after-hour services. These employers may require locksmiths to answer service calls at any time of the day or night, including weekends.

Locksmiths stand during much of their working time, but they also often need to crouch, bend, stoop, and kneel. Sometimes they are required to lift heavy gates, doors, and other objects when dealing with safes, strong rooms, or lock fittings.

Locksmith workshops are usually well lit, well heated, and well ventilated. Some shops, particularly mobile ones, however, may be crowded and small, requiring that workers move carefully around fixtures and stock. Some locksmiths work outdoors, installing or repairing protective or warning devices. Some workers who work at other sites may have to do considerable driving. Locksmiths may work alone or may be required at times to work with others at stores, banks, factories, schools, and other facilities. Physical injuries are not common, but minor ones can occur from soldering irons, welding equipment, electric shocks, flying bits from grinders, and sharp lock or key edges.

Outlook

There are approximately 27,000 locksmiths employed in the United States, in small and large shops, as well as in-house for other businesses. This number is expected to grow about as fast as the average through 2008.

Population growth and an expanding public awareness of the need for preventive measures against home, business, and auto burglary continue to create needs for security devices and their maintenance. Also, many individuals and firms are replacing older lock and alarm systems with the latest developments in computerized equipment. Consequently, opportunities will be best for those workers who are able to install and service electronic security systems.

The locksmith trade itself has remained stable, with few economic fluctuations, and locksmiths with an extensive knowledge of their trade are rarely unemployed.

For More Information

For information on schools and colleges that offer locksmith classes, contact:

Accrediting Commission of Career Schools and Colleges of Technology
2101 Wilson Boulevard, Suite 302
Arlington, VA 22201
Tel: 703-247-4212
Email: info@accsct.org
Web: http://www.accsct.org/

For information on locksmithing careers, certification, continuing education, and scholarships, contact:

Associated Locksmiths of America
3003 Live Oak Street
Dallas, TX 75204
Tel: 800-532-2562
Email: aloa@aloa.org
Web: http://www.aloa.org

For a list of accredited home-study programs in locksmithing, contact:

Distance Education and Training Council
1601 18th Street, NW
Washington, DC 20009-2529
Tel: 202-234-5100
Email: detc@detc.org
Web: http://www.detc.org/

Nannies

Family and consumer science Psychology	School Subjects
Communication/ideas Helping/teaching	Personal Skills
Primarily indoors Primarily one location	Work Environment
High school diploma	Minimum Education Level
$7,800 to $14,300 to $20,800+	Salary Range
Voluntary	Certification or Licensing
Much faster than the average	Outlook

Overview

Nannies, also known as *au pairs,* are caregivers who care for children in the parents' homes. The children usually range in age from infant to 11 years old. The nanny's responsibilities may include supervising the nursery, organizing play activities, taking the children to appointments or classes, and keeping the children's quarters clean and intact. They may be responsible for supervising the child part of the day or the entire day.

In a large and growing percentage of American families, both parents hold full-time jobs and require full-time child care, which has resulted in increased employment opportunities for nannies. In many other families, parents are opting for part-time work or running businesses out of their homes. Although this allows the parents to be with their children more than if they worked a traditional job, the unpredictability of children's needs makes a nanny's help welcome. A growing segment of parents prefer that their children be cared for at home as opposed to taking them to a day care facility. Thus, the nanny has become a viable and often satisfactory solution. There are over 300,000 child care workers employed in private homes.

History

Nannies have been a staple of European staffs for hundreds of years, often epitomizing the upper-class British childhood. They have captured our imaginations and have been the basis for fictional characters ranging from Jane Eyre to Mary Poppins. In the United States, nannies or nursemaids have worked in the homes of the very wealthy for centuries. Only quite recently, however, has the role of the nanny entered into the lives of the middle class.

Because of the steadily increasing demand for highly skilled, reliable, private child care, nannies have gained such popularity that schools have sprung up across the country to train and place them. However, the vast majority of nannies come from overseas. Young women and men from the West Indies, the Philippines, Ireland, South Central America, and other regions often immigrate to the United States to become nannies because of the poor economic conditions in their own countries. These nannies are often taken advantage of by the people they work for. They may be paid next to nothing, expected to be completely at the disposal of the family, even at a moment's notice, and usually receive no health insurance or other benefits. Unfortunately, they put up with this sort of treatment mainly because they are afraid to lose the income, a large part of which they often send home to relatives in their native country.

With proper training and placement, however, nannies can find their jobs to be pleasant, satisfying experiences.

The Job

Nannies perform their child care duties in the homes of the families that employ them. Unlike other kinds of household help, nannies are specifically concerned with the needs of the children in their charge. Nannies prepare the children's meals, making sure they are nutritious, appealing, and appetizing. They may do grocery shopping specifically for the children. Nannies may attend the children during their mealtimes and oversee their training in table manners and proper etiquette. They also clean up after the children's meals. If there is an infant in the family, a nanny will wash and sterilize bottles and feed the infant. It is not part of a nanny's regular duties to cook for the adult members of the household or do domestic chores outside of those required for the children.

Nannies are responsible for keeping order in the children's quarters. They may clean the bedrooms, nursery, and playrooms, making sure beds are made with clean linens and sufficient blankets. Nannies may also wash and iron the children's clothing and do any necessary mending. They make sure that the clothing is neatly put away. With older children, the nanny may begin instructions in orderliness and neatness, teaching children how to organize their possessions.

Nannies bathe and dress the children and instill proper grooming skills. Children often seek the assistance of their nanny in getting ready for family parties or holidays. As the children get older, nannies help them learn how to dress themselves and take care of their appearance.

Not only are nannies responsible for the care and training of their charges, but they also act as companions and guardians. They plan games and learning activities for the children and supervise their play, encouraging fairness and good sportsmanship. They may be responsible for planning activities to commemorate holidays, special events, or birthdays. These activities may center on field trips, arts and crafts, or parties. Nannies may travel with families on trips and vacations or they may take the children on short excursions without their families. Nannies must be detail oriented when it comes to the children entrusted to their care. They keep records of illnesses, allergies, and injuries. They also note learning skills and related progress as well as personal achievements, such as abilities in games or arts and crafts. Later, they relate these events and achievements to the parents.

Nannies act as the parents' assistants by focusing closely on the children and fostering the behavior expected of them. They are responsible for carrying out the parents' directions for care and activities. By setting good examples and helping the children follow guidelines established by their parents, nannies encourage the development of happy and confident personalities.

Requirements

High School

From an educational standpoint, nannies usually are required to have at least a high school diploma or equivalent (GED). Helpful high school classes include health, psychology, and home economics. English and communication classes also are useful as they provide skills that will help in everyday dealings with the children and their parents. Nannies usually must also have a valid driver's license since they may be asked to chauffeur the children to doctors' appointments or other outings.

Postsecondary Training

There are several schools that offer specialized nanny training usually lasting between 12 and 16 weeks. These programs are typically accredited by individual state agencies. Employers generally prefer applicants who have completed an accredited program. Graduates of accredited programs also can command higher salaries.

Two- and four-year programs are available at many colleges and include courses on early childhood education, child growth and development, and child care. College course work in nanny training may also focus on communication, family health, first aid, child psychology, and food and nutrition. Classes may include play and recreational games, arts and crafts, children's literature, and safety and health. Because nannies may be responsible for children of various ages, the course work focuses on each stage of childhood development and the particular needs of individual children. Special emphasis is given to the care of infants. Professional nanny schools may also give instruction on family management, personal appearance, and appropriate conduct.

Certification or Licensing

Although nannies are not required to be certified, completing a program that offers you certification—earning the title, Certified Professional Nanny—will be to your benefit. Certification shows potential employers your commitment to the work as well as your level of training.

Other Requirements

Nannies must possess an even and generous temperament when working with children. They must be kind, affectionate, and genuinely interested in the child's well-being and development. Good physical condition, energy, and stamina are also necessary for success in this career. Nannies must be able to work well on their own initiative and have sound judgment to handle any small crises or emergencies that arise. They must know how to instill discipline and carry out the parents' expectations.

They should be loyal and committed to the children and respect the families for whom they work. In some cases, this is difficult, since nannies are often privy to negative elements of family life, including the emotional problems of parents and their neglect of their children. Nannies need to recognize that they are not part of the family and should not allow themselves to become too familiar with its members. When they disagree with the family on matters of raising the children, they should do so with tact and the realization that they are only employees. Finally, it is imperative that they be discreet about confidential family matters. A nanny who gossips about family affairs is likely to be rapidly dismissed.

Exploring

Babysitting is an excellent way to gain child care experience. Often, a *babysitter* cares for children without any supervision, thereby learning child management and personal responsibility. Volunteer or part-time work at day care centers, nurseries, or elementary schools can also be beneficial.

Talk to a nanny to get further information. There are several placement agencies for prospective nannies, and one of them might be able to set up a meeting or phone interview with someone who works in the field.

Gather information about nannies either from the library or from sources listed at the end of this article.

Employers

Private household workers hold approximately 928,000 jobs in the United States; 33 percent are child care workers. Mid- to upper-income parents who seek in-home child care for their children usually employ nannies. These opportunities are generally available across the country in large cities and affluent suburbs. Most nannies are placed in homes by placement agencies, employment agencies, or through government authorized programs.

Starting Out

Most schools that train nannies offer placement services. In addition, it is possible to register with an employment agency that places child care workers. Currently, there are over 200 agencies that specialize in placing nannies. Some agencies conduct recruitment drives or fairs to find applicants. Newspaper classified ads may also list job openings for nannies.

Prospective nannies should screen potential employers carefully. Applicants should ask for references from previous nannies, particularly if a family has had many prior nannies, and talk with one or more of them, if possible. There are many horror stories in nanny circles about past employers, and the prospective worker should not assume that every employer is exactly as he or she appears to be at first. Nannies also need to make sure that the specific duties and terms of the job are explicitly specified in a contract. Most agencies will supply sample contracts.

Advancement

Over half of the nannies working in this country are under the age of 30. Many nannies work in child care temporarily as a way to support themselves through school. Many nannies leave their employers to start families of their own. Some nannies, as their charges grow older and start school, may be employed by a new family every few years. This may result in better paying positions.

Other advancement opportunities for nannies depend on the personal initiative of the nanny. Some nannies enroll in college to get the necessary training to become teachers or child psychologists. Other nannies may establish their own child care agencies or schools for nannies.

Earnings

A nanny's salary can range from $150 to $400 or more per week, which translates into a yearly salary of $7,800 to $20,800 or more. This range is based on a five-day workweek of as many as 60 hours. Nannies almost always work more than 40 hours per week, so clearly those on the lower end of the pay scale are rather poorly compensated for their time. This salary range also depends on such factors as the number of children, length of time with a family, and level of previous experience. Some employers provide room and board. Presently, the highest demands for nannies are in large cities on the west and east coasts. High demand can result in higher wages.

Some nannies may be asked to travel with the family. If it is a business-oriented trip, a nanny may be compensated with wages as well as additional days off upon return. If the travel is for vacation, a nanny may get paid a bonus for working additional days. Some employers choose not to take their nannies along when they travel, and these nannies may not earn any wages while the family is gone. Such situations can be a financial disadvantage for the nanny who has been promised full-time work and full-time pay. It is recommended that nannies anticipate possible scenarios or situations that may affect their working schedules and wages and discuss these issues with employers in advance.

Nannies often have work contracts with their families that designate wages, requirements, fringe benefits, and salary increases. Health insurance, worker's compensation, and Social Security tax are sometimes included in the benefits package. Annual pay raises vary, with increases of 7 or 8 percent being on the high end of the scale.

Work Environment

No other job involves as intimate a relationship with other people and their children as the nanny's job. Because nannies often live with their employers, it is important that they choose their employer with as much care as the employer chooses them. All necessary working conditions need to be negotiated at the time of hire. Nannies should be fair, flexible, and able to adapt to changes easily. Because nannies work in their employers' homes, their working conditions vary greatly. Some nannies are live-ins, sharing the home of their employer because of convenience or because of the number or age of children in the family. Newborn babies require additional care that may require the nanny to live on the premises.

It is also common for nannies to live with their families during the week and return to their homes on the weekends. When nannies live in the family's home, they usually have their own quarters or a small apartment that is separate from the rest of the family's bedrooms and offers some privacy. Sometimes the nanny's room is next to the children's room so it is possible for the nanny to respond immediately if help is needed.

Nannies who are not live-ins may expect to stay at the home for long periods of time, much longer than a traditional nine-to-five job. Since it often is the nanny's responsibility to put the children to bed in the evening, a nanny may not return home until late evening. Often nannies are asked to stay late or work weekends if the parents have other engagements.

The work of a nanny can often be stressful or unpleasant. Many employers expect their nannies to do things unrelated to their job, such as clean the house, run errands, walk dogs, or babysit for neighborhood children. Some employers may be condescending, rude, and critical. Some mothers, while they need and want the services of a nanny, grow resentful and jealous of the bonds the nanny forms with the children.

Nannies have very few legal rights with regard to their jobs and have little recourse to deal with unfair employers. Job security is very poor as parents have less need for nannies as their children get older and start school. In addition, nannies are often fired with no notice and sometimes no explanation due to the whims of their employers. Leaving behind a job and the children they have taken care of and grown close to can be emotionally difficult for workers in this field.

The work is often strenuous, requiring a great deal of lifting, standing, and walking or running. The work is also mentally taxing as young children demand constant attention and energy. However, it can be very rewarding for nannies as they grow close to the children, helping with their upbringing and care. In the best cases, the nanny becomes an integral part of the family he or she works for and is treated with professionalism, respect, and appreciation.

Outlook

The continuing trend of both parents working outside the home ensures that nannies will remain in demand. Even if many of these parents switch to part-time jobs, there will still be a need for qualified child care providers. Presently, the demand for nannies outweighs the supply, and graduating nannies may find themselves faced with several job offers. In addition, the long hours and low pay, make for a high turnover rate in this field, and replacement workers are in steady demand. It may be years before the gap between the number of positions open and the availability of nannies diminishes.

For More Information

For information on training, accredited programs, and careers as a nanny, contact the following organizations:

American Council of Nanny Schools
Delta College, Room A-67
University Center, MI 48710
Tel: 517-686-9417

English Nanny and Governess School
30 South Franklin Street
Chagrin Falls, OH 44022
Tel: 800-733-1984
Email: school@nanny-governess.com
Web: http://www.nanny-governess.com

International Nanny Association
900 Haddon Avenue, Suite 438
Collingswood, NJ 08108
Tel: 856-858-0808
Web: http://www.nanny.org

The following organization is an exchange program that places foreign students between the ages of 18 and 26 in American homes as au pairs for one year. For more information, contact:

GoAuPair
6965 Union Park Center, Suite 100
Midvale, UT 84047
Tel: 888-287-2471
Web: http://www.goaupair.com

The following organization is a national support group run by nannies for nannies. For information on their national network, newsletters, and yearly conferences, contact:

National Association of Nannies
PMB 2004
25 Route 31 South, Suite C
Pennington, NJ 08534
Tel: 800-344-6266
Email: NANannies@aol.com
Web: http://www.nannyassociation.com

Personal Shoppers

	School Subjects
Business	
Family and consumer science	

	Personal Skills
Following instructions	
Helping/teaching	

	Work Environment
Primarily indoors	
Primarily multiple locations	

	Minimum Education Level
High school diploma	

	Salary Range
$10,000 to $22,000 to $38,000	

	Certification or Licensing
None available	

	Outlook
About as fast as the average	

Overview

People who don't have the time or the ability to go shopping for clothes, gifts, groceries, and other items use the services of *personal shoppers*. Personal shoppers shop department stores, look at catalogs, and surf the Internet for the best buys and most appropriate items for their clients. Relying on a sense of style and an ability to spot a bargain, a personal shopper helps clients develop a wardrobe and find gifts for friends, relatives, and employees. Though personal shoppers work all across the country, their services are in most demand in large, metropolitan areas.

History

For decades, American retailers have been working to create easier ways to shop. Mail-order was an early innovation—catalog companies like Montgomery Wards and Sears and Roebuck started business in the late 19th century to meet the shopping needs of people living in rural areas and small towns. Many consumers relied on mail-order for everything from suits and dresses to furniture and stoves; Sears even sold automobiles through the mail. Shopping for food, clothes, and gifts was considered a household chore, a responsibility that belonged to women. By the late 1800s, shopping had developed into a popular pastime in metropolitan areas. Wealthy women of leisure turned downtown shopping districts into the busiest sections of their cities, as department stores, boutiques, tea shops, and cafes evolved to serve them.

As more women joined the work force after World War II, retailers worked to make their shopping areas more convenient. Supermarkets, shopping centers, and malls became popular. Toward the end of the 20th century, shoppers began looking for even more simplicity and convenience. In the 1990s, many companies began to market their products via the Internet. In addition to Internet commerce, overworked men and women are turning to personal shoppers, professional organizers, and personal assistants to fulfill their shopping needs.

The Job

Looking for a job where you get to shop all the time, tell people what to wear, and spend somebody else's money? Though this may seem to describe the life of the personal shopper, it's not quite accurate. For one thing, personal shoppers don't get to shop all the time—they will be spending some time in stores and browsing catalogs, but they're often looking for something very specific, and working as quickly as they can. And they do not so much tell people what to wear, as teach them how to best match outfits, what colors suit them, and what styles are most appropriate for their workplaces. And, yes, personal shoppers spend someone else's money, but it's all for someone else's closet. So, if you're not too disillusioned, read on: working as a personal shopper may still be right for you.

Personal shoppers help people who are unable or uninterested in doing their own shopping. They are hired to look for that perfect gift for a difficult-to-please aunt. Or by senior citizens, or people with disabilities, to do their grocery shopping and run other shopping errands. Personal shoppers help professionals create a nice, complete wardrobe. All the while, they rely on their knowledge of the local marketplace in order to do the shopping quickly and efficiently.

Some personal shoppers use their backgrounds in other areas to assist clients. Someone with a background in real estate may serve as a personal shopper for houses, working for a buyer rather than a seller. These *house shoppers* inspect houses and do some of the client's bargaining. Those with a background in cosmetology may work as *image consultants,* advising clients on their hair, clothes, and makeup. Another shopper may have some experience in dealing antiques, and will help clients locate particular items. An *interior decorator* may shop for furniture and art to decorate a home.

Personal shoppers who offer wardrobe consultation will need to visit their client's home and evaluate his or her clothes. They help their clients determine what additional clothes and accessories they'll need, and they advise them on what jackets to wear with what pants, what skirt to wear with what blouse. Together with their client, personal shoppers determine what additional clothes are needed to complete the wardrobe, and they come up with a budget. Then it's off to the stores.

Irene Kato owns I Kan Do It, a personal shopping service. She offers a variety of services, including at-home wardrobe consultation, closet organization, and gift shopping. "Most of my shopping so far has been for clothes," Kato says. "I have a fairly good idea of what I'm looking for so I don't spend too much time in any one store if I don't see what I want right away. I can usually find two or three choices for my client and rarely have to shop another day." Kato spends about two to three hours every other day shopping, and spends about two hours a day in her office working on publicity, her budget, and corresponding with clients. Shopping for one client can take about three hours. "I have always enjoyed shopping," Kato says, "and especially like finding bargains. Waiting in lines, crowds, etc., does not bother me."

Personal shoppers often cater to professionals needing business attire and wardrobe consultation. A smaller part of their business will be shopping for gifts. They may even supplement their business by running other errands, such as purchasing theater tickets, making deliveries, and going to the post office. Many personal shoppers also work as *professional organizers:* they go into homes and offices to organize desks, kitchens, and closets.

In addition to the actual shopping, personal shoppers have administrative responsibilities. They must keep business records, make phone calls, and schedule appointments. Since personal shopping is a fairly new endeavor, personal shoppers must be expert at educating the public about their services. "A personal shopper has no commodity to sell," Kato says, "only themselves. So it is twice as hard to attract clients." To publicize her business, Irene maintains a Web site that lists the services she provides and testimonials from clients. She also belongs to two professional organizations that help her network and develop her business: Executive Women International and Giving Referrals to Other Women.

Requirements

High School

Take classes in home economics to develop budget and consumer skills, as well as learn about fashion and home design. If the class offers a sewing unit, you'll learn about tailoring, and can develop an eye for clothes sizes. Math, business, and accounting courses will prepare you for the administrative details of the job. English composition and speech classes will help you develop the communication skills you'll need for promoting your business, and for advising clients about their wardrobes.

Postsecondary Training

Many people working as personal shoppers have had experience in other areas of business. They've worked as managers in corporations or have worked as salespeople in retail stores. But because of the entrepreneurial nature of the career, you don't need any specific kind of education or training. A small-business course at your local community college, along with classes in design, fashion, and consumer science, can help you develop the skills you'll need for the job. If you're unfamiliar with the computer, you should take some classes to learn desktop publishing programs for creating business cards and other publicity material.

Other Requirements

"I seem to have an empathy for people," Irene Kato says. "After talking with a client I know what they want and what they're looking for. I am a very good listener." In addition to these people skills, a personal shopper should be patient, and capable of dealing with the long lines and customer service of department stores. You should be creative, and able to come up with a variety of gift ideas. A sense of style is important, along with knowledge of the latest brands and designers. You'll need a good eye for colors and fabrics. You should also be well-dressed and organized so that your client will know to trust your wardrobe suggestions.

Exploring

If you've spent any time at the mall, you probably already have enough shopping experience. And if you've had to buy clothes and gifts with limited funds, then you know something about budgeting. Sign up for the services of a personal shopper in a department store; in most stores the service is free, and you'll get a sense of how a shopper works. Pay close attention to the information they request from you in the beginning, then ask them later about their decision-making process. Irene Kato advises future personal shoppers to work a few years at a retail clothing store. "This way," she says, "you can observe the way people dress, what shapes and sizes we all are, how fashion trends come and go, and what stays."

Employers

Professional men and women with high incomes and busy schedules are the primary employers of personal shoppers. They may also work with people with new jobs requiring dress clothes, but also with people who need to perk up an old wardrobe. Personal shoppers may work for executives in corporations who need to buy gifts for large staffs of employees. Some of their clients may be elderly or have disabilities and have problems getting out to do their shopping.

Starting Out

The start-up costs can be very low; you may only have to invest in a computer, business cards, and a reliable form of transportation. But it could take you a very long time to develop a regular clientele. You'll want to develop the business part-time while still working full-time at another, more reliable job. Some of your first clients may come from your workplace. Offer free introductory services to a few people and encourage them to spread the word around and hand out your business card. You'll also need to become very familiar with the local retail establishments and the discount stores with low-cost, high quality merchandise.

"My friends and colleagues at work," Irene Kato says, "were always complimentary on what I wore and would ask where I bought my clothes, where they could find certain items, where were the best sales." Kato was taking the part-time approach to developing her personal shopping service, when downsizing at her company thrust her into the new business earlier than she'd planned. She had the opportunity to take an entrepreneur class at a local private university which helped her devise a business plan and taught her about the pros and cons of starting a business.

Advancement

It takes years of dedication, quality work, and referrals to create a successful business. Personal shoppers should expect lean early years as they work to build their business and expand their clientele. After a few years of working part-time and providing superior service, a personal shopper may develop his or her business into a full-time endeavor. Eventually, they may be able to hire an assistant to help them with the administrative work, such as client billing and scheduling.

Earnings

Personal shoppers bill their clients in different ways: they set a regular fee for services, charge a percentage of the sale, or charge an hourly rate. They might use all these methods in their business; their billing method may depend on the client and the service. For example, when offering wardrobe consultation and shopping for clothes, a personal shopper may find it best to charge by the hour; when shopping for a small gift, it may be more reasonable to only charge a percentage. Personal shoppers charge anywhere from $25 to $125 an hour; the average hourly rate is about $75. Successful shoppers living in a large city can make between $1,500 and $3,000 a month.

Work Environment

Personal shoppers have all the advantages of owning their own business, including setting their own hours, and keeping a flexible schedule. But they also have all the disadvantages, such as job insecurity and lack of benefits. "I have a bad habit of thinking about my business almost constantly," Irene says. Though personal shoppers don't have to deal with the stress of a full-time office job, they will have the stress of finding new clients and keeping the business afloat entirely by themselves.

Although personal shoppers usually work from a home office, they still spend a lot of time with people, from clients to salespeople. They will obviously spend some time in department stores; if they like to shop, this can be enjoyable even when they're not buying anything for themselves. In some cases, personal shoppers visit clients' homes to advise them on their wardrobe. They do a lot of traveling, driving to a department store after a meeting with a client, then back to the client's with the goods.

Outlook

Personal shopping is a new business development, so anyone embarking on the career will be taking some serious risks. There's not a lot of research available about the career, no national professional organization specifically serving personal shoppers, and no real sense of the career's future. The success of Internet commerce will probably have a big effect on the future of personal shopping. If purchasing items through the Internet becomes more commonplace, personal shoppers may have to establish places for themselves on the World Wide Web. Some personal shoppers currently with Web sites offer consultation via email and help people purchase products online.

To attract the widest variety of clients, personal shoppers should offer as expansive a service as they can. Professional organizing is being recognized as one of the top home businesses for the future; the membership for the National Association of Professional Organizers has doubled every year since 1985. Personal assistants, those who run errands for others, have also caught the attention of industry experts, and programs are available to assist people interested in entering this field.

For More Information

For more information on professional networking opportunities for women, contact:

Executive Women International
515 South 700 East, Suite 2A
Salt Lake City, UT 84102
Tel: 888-EWI-1229
Email: ewi@executivewomen.org
Web: http://www.executivewomen.org/

To learn about careers as professional organizers, contact:

National Association of Professional Organizers
PO Box 140647
Austin, TX 78714
Tel: 512-206-0151
Web: http://www.napo.net

For more information on personal shoppers, check out the following Web site:

I Kan Do It
http://www.sowashco.com/ikandoit

Personal Trainers

	School Subjects
Health	
Physical education	

	Personal Skills
Communication/ideas	
Helping/teaching	

	Work Environment
Primarily indoors	
Primarily multiple locations	

	Minimum Education Level
Some postsecondary training	

	Salary Range
$20/hour to $40/hour	
to $100/hour	

	Certification or Licensing
Voluntary	

	Outlook
Faster than the average	

Overview

Personal trainers, often known as *fitness trainers,* assist health-conscious people with exercise, weight training, weight loss, diet and nutrition, and medical rehabilitation. During one training session, or over a period of several sessions, trainers teach their clients how to achieve their health and fitness goals. They train in the homes of their clients, their own studio spaces, or in health clubs. Approximately 62,000 personal trainers work in the United States, either independently or on the staff of a fitness center.

History

For much of the last half of the 20th century, "98-pound weaklings" were tempted by the Charles Atlas comic book ads to buy his workout plan and to bulk up. Atlas capitalized on a concern for good health that developed into the fitness industry after World War II. Though physical fitness has always been important to the human body, things have changed quite a bit since the days when people had to chase and hunt their own food. Before the industrial revolution, people were much more active, and the need for supplemental exercise was unnecessary. But the last century has brought easier living, laziness, and processed snack foods.

Even as early as the late 1800s, people became concerned about their health and weight and began to flock to spas and exercise camps. This proved to be a passing fad for the most part, but medical and nutritional study began to carefully explore the significance of exercise. During World War II, rehabilitation medicine proved more effective than extended rest in returning soldiers to the front line. Even the early days of TV featured many morning segments devoted to exercise. The videotape revolution of the 1980s went hand in hand with a new fitness craze, as Jane Fonda's workout tape became a bestseller and inspired a whole industry of fitness tapes and books. Now most health clubs offer the services of fitness trainers to attend to the personal health concerns of its members.

The Job

Remember the first time you ever went to the gym? The weight machines resembled medieval forms of torture, and the buff bodybuilders loitered about, as if it was their job to be in better shape than everybody else. So, to avoid the weight training, you stuck to the treadmill, running like a gerbil on caffeine. Or maybe you called upon the services of a personal trainer. If you have worked with a personal trainer, then you've learned a great deal about your own health and fitness: you've learned how to properly use weight machines; you've learned about calisthenics and cardiovascular exercise; you've developed a proper diet for yourself. If you've reached your own workout goals, then you may be ready to help others reach theirs.

"You have to believe in working out and eating healthy," advises Emelina Edwards, a personal trainer in New Orleans. For 12 years she's been in the business of personal training, a career she chose after whipping herself into great shape at the age of 46. Now, at 58, she has a lot of first-hand experience in training, nutrition, aerobic exercise, and stress management. Emelina says, "You have to practice what you preach."

And practice, Edwards does—not only does she devote time every day to her own weight training, jogging, and meditation, but she works with three to five clients in the workout facility in her home. She has a total of about 20 clients, some of whom she assists in one-on-one sessions, and others in small groups. Her clients have included men and women from the ages of 20 to 80 who are looking to improve their general physical condition, or to work on specific ailments. When meeting with a client for the first time, Edwards gets a quick history of physical problems and medical conditions. "If the problems are serious," she says, "I check with their doctor. If mild, I explain to them what I believe will help." When she discovered that four out of five people seeking her help suffered from back problems, she did a great deal of research on back pain and how to alleviate it through exercise. "I teach people how to do for themselves," she says. "Sometimes I see a person once, or for three or four sessions, or forever."

In addition to working directly with clients, Edwards is active promoting her line of "Total Body Rejuvenation" products. These products, consisting of audio tapes and books, are based on her years of experience and the many articles she has written for fitness publications. A recent appearance on the popular Spanish talk show "Christina" has resulted in a number of calls that Edwards has had to handle herself. When she's not training clients, writing articles, and selling products, she's reading fitness publications to keep up on the business, as well as speaking at public events. "When I realized I loved training," she says, "I thought of all the things I could relate to it. So along with the training, I began to write about it, and to give talks on health and fitness."

Successful personal trainers don't necessarily have to keep as busy as Edwards. They may choose to specialize in certain areas of personal training. They may work as an *athletic trainer,* helping athletes prepare for sports activities. They may specialize in helping with the rehabilitation treatment of people with injuries and other physical problems. Yoga, dance, martial arts, indoor cycling, boxing, and water fitness have all become aspects of special training programs. People call upon the aid of personal trainers to help them quit smoking, to assist with healthy pregnancies, and to maintain mental and emotional stability. Whatever the problem, whether mental or physical, people are turning to exercise and nutrition to help them deal with it.

Many personal trainers have their own studios or home gyms where they train their clients; others go into the homes of their clients. Because of the demands of the workplace, many personal trainers also work in offices and corporate fitness centers. Though most health clubs hire their own trainers to assist with club members, some hire freelance trainers as independent contractors. These independent contractors are not considered staff members and don't receive employee benefits. IDEA, a fitness professional association, found that 30 percent of the personal trainers hired by the fitness centers surveyed were independent contractors.

Requirements

High School

If you're interested in health and fitness, you're probably already taking physical education classes and involved in sports activities. It's also important to take health courses and courses like home economics, which include lessons in diet and nutrition. Business courses can help you prepare for the management aspect of running your own personal training service. Science courses such as biology, chemistry, and physiology are important for your understanding of muscle groups, food and drug reactions, and other concerns of exercise science. If you're not interested in playing on sports teams, you may be able to volunteer as an assistant—you'll learn about athletic training, as well as rehabilitation treatments.

Postsecondary Training

A college education isn't required to work as a personal trainer, but you can benefit from one of the many fitness-related programs offered at colleges across the country. Some relevant college programs are: health education, exercise and sports science, fitness program management, and athletic training. These programs include courses in therapeutic exercise, nutrition, aerobics, and fitness and aging. IDEA recommends a bachelor's degree from a program that includes at least a semester each in anatomy, kinesiology, and exercise physiology. IDEA has some scholarships available to students seeking careers as fitness professionals.

If you're not interested in a full four-year program, many schools offer shorter versions of their bachelor's programs. Upon completing a shorter program, you'll receive either an associate's degree or certification from the school. Once you've established yourself in the business, continuing education courses are important for you to keep up with the advances in the industry. IDEA is one of many organizations that offer independent study courses, conferences, and seminars.

Certification or Licensing

There are so many schools and organizations that offer certification to personal trainers that it has become a concern in the industry. Without more rigid standards, the profession could suffer at the hands of less experienced, less skilled trainers. Some organizations only require membership fees and short tests for certification. Emelina Edwards isn't certified and doesn't believe that certification is necessary. "Experience is what counts," she says.

But some health clubs look for certified trainers when hiring independent contractors. If you are seeking certification, you should choose a certifying board that offers scientifically based exams and requires continuing education credits. American Council on Exercise, the National Federation of Professional Trainers, and American Fitness Professionals and Associates are just a few of the many groups with certification programs.

Other Requirements

Physical fitness and knowledge of health and nutrition are the most important assets of personal trainers. "The more intelligently you can speak to someone," Edwards says, "the more receptive they'll be." Your clients will also be more receptive to patience and friendliness. "I'm very enthusiastic and positive," she says regarding the way she works with her clients. You should be able to explain things clearly, as well as recognize progress and encourage it. You should be comfortable working one-on-one with people of all ages and in all physical conditions. An interest in reading fitness books and publications is important to your continuing education.

Exploring

Your high school may have a weight-training program, or some other extracurricular fitness program, as part of the athletic department—in addition to signing up for the program, assist the faculty who manage it. That way, you can learn about what goes into developing and maintaining such a program. If your school doesn't have a fitness program, seek one out at a community center, or join a health club. You should also try the services of a personal trainer. By conditioning yourself and eating a healthy diet, you'll get a good sense of the duties of a personal trainer. Any number of books and magazines address issues of health and nutrition and offer weight training advice. A magazine specifically for personal trainers is published 10 times a year by IDEA. Seek out part-time work at a gym or health club, and you'll meet trainers and learn about weight machines and certification programs.

Employers

IDEA reports that there are approximately 62,000 personal trainers working in the United States. Personal trainers are employed by people of all ages. Individuals hire the services of trainers, as do companies for the benefit of their employees. Though most health clubs hire personal trainers full-time, a large percentage of clubs hire trainers on an independent contractor basis. Sports and exercise programs at community colleges hire trainers part-time to conduct classes.

Personal trainers can find clients in most major cities in all regions of the country. In addition to health clubs and corporate fitness centers, trainers find work at YMCAs, aerobics studios, and hospital fitness centers.

Starting Out

Most people who begin personal training do so after successful experiences with their own training. Once they've developed a good exercise regimen and healthy diet plan for themselves, they may feel ready to help others. Emelina Edwards had hit a low point in her life, following a divorce and money problems, and had turned to weight training to help her get through the difficult times. "I didn't have a college degree," she says, "and I needed something to do. All I had was weight training." She then called up all the women she knew, promoting her services as a personal trainer. Through the benefit of word-of-mouth, Edwards built up a clientele.

Some trainers begin by working part-time or full-time for health clubs and, after making connections, they go into business for themselves. As with most small businesses, personal trainers must promote themselves through classified ads, flyers posted in community centers, and other forms of advertisement. Many personal trainers have published guides on how to establish businesses. IDEA offers a package called "The Business of Personal Training," which includes a textbook and audio cassettes with advice on selling and marketing services, developing networking skills, and creating partnerships with retailers, medical professionals, and others.

Advancement

After personal trainers have taken on as many individual clients as they need to maintain a business, they may choose to lead small group training sessions or conduct large aerobics classes. Some trainers join forces with other trainers to start their own fitness centers. Trainers who are employed by fitness centers may be promoted to the position of personal training director. These workers supervise and schedule other personal trainers and manage department budgets.

Edwards has advanced her business by venturing out into other areas of fitness instruction, such as publishing books and speaking to groups. "I want to develop more in the public speaking arena," she says. Right now, she only speaks to local groups—she'd like to go national. "I'd also like to break into the Latin market," she says. "The interest is there, and the response has been great."

Earnings

A compensation survey conducted by IDEA in 2000 reports that personal trainers who worked for health clubs and other fitness centers earned an average of $23 an hour. The top four factors determining pay were degree/certification, specialty area expertise, continuing education, and years in the industry. Personal trainers who offer specialized instruction (such as in yoga, martial arts, or indoor cycling) earned an average of $20 an hour. Personal training directors, who supervise other personal trainers, earned an annual salary of $25,500.

Personal trainers who work with their own clients in their own homes can charge a higher hourly rate. The average hourly fee for the services of personal trainers is $40 to $100.

Work Environment

Personal training is obviously a physically demanding job, but anybody who is in good shape and who eats a healthy diet should be able to handle the demands. Personal trainers who work out of their homes will enjoy familiar and comfortable surroundings. Trainers who work in a gym as independent contractors will also experience a comfortable workplace. Most good gyms maintain a cool temperature, keep the facilities clean and well-lit, and care for the weight machines. Whether in a gym or at home, personal trainers work directly with their clients, usually in one-on-one training sessions. In this teaching situation, the workplace is usually quiet and conducive to learning.

As with most self-employment, sustaining a business can be both rewarding and difficult. Many trainers appreciate being able to keep their own hours, and to work as little, or as much, as they care to. By setting their own schedules, they can arrange time for their personal workout routines. But, without an employer, there's less security, no benefits, and no steady paycheck. Personal trainers have to regularly promote their services and be ready to take on new clients.

Outlook

Fitness training will continue to enjoy strong growth in the near future. As the baby boomers grow older, they will increasingly rely on the services of personal trainers. Boomers have long been interested in health and fitness, and they'll carry this into their old age. A knowledge of special weight training, stretching exercises, and diets for seniors will be necessary for personal trainers in the years to come. Trainers will actively promote their services to senior centers and retirement communities.

With the growing number of health publications and fitness centers available to the public, people are much more knowledgeable about exercise and nutrition. This could increase business for personal trainers as people better understand the necessity of proper training and seek out professional assistance. Trainers may also be going into more of their clients homes as people set up their own workout stations complete with weights and treadmills. In the health and medical field, new developments are constantly affecting how people eat and exercise. Personal trainers must keep up with these advances, as well as any new trends in fitness and dieting.

For More Information

For general health and fitness topics, and to learn about certification, contact the following organizations:

American Council on Exercise
5820 Oberlin Drive, Suite 102
San Diego, CA 92121-3787
Tel: 619-535-8227
Web: http://www.acefitness.org

American Fitness Professionals and Associates
PO Box 214
Ship Bottom, NJ 08008
Tel: 609-978-7583
Email: afpa@afpafitness.com
Web: http://www.afpafitness.com/

National Federation of Professional Trainers
PO Box 4579
Lafayette, IN 47903-4579
Tel: 800-729-6378
Email: info@nfpt.com
Web: http://www.nfpt.com/

IDEA conducts surveys, provides continuing education, and publishes a number of books and magazines relevant to the business. For information about the fitness industry in general, and personal training specifically, contact:

IDEA, Inc.
6190 Cornerstone Court East, Suite 204
San Diego, CA 92121-3773
Tel: 800-999-4332, ext. 7
Email: nonmemberquestions@ideafit.com
Web: http://www.ideafit.com

Pest Control Workers

Chemistry Mathematics	School Subjects
Following instructions Technical/scientific	Personal Skills
Indoors and outdoors Primarily multiple locations	Work Environment
High school diploma	Minimum Education Level
$10,400 to $18,300 to $32,590+	Salary Range
Required by certain states	Certification or Licensing
Faster than the average	Outlook

Overview

Pest control workers treat residential and commercial properties with chemicals and mechanical traps to get rid of rodents, insects, and other common pests. They may work for a pest control company, lawn or landscaping firms, or own and operate their own company. Pest control workers make periodic visits to their clients' properties to make sure they remain pest-free. They may also use chemicals to control diseases and pests that attack lawns, shrubs, and other outdoor vegetation. There are approximately 52,000 pest control workers in the United States.

History

Pest control as an industry is a fairly recent development. In earlier times, fumigators were often brought into houses where someone had suffered a highly contagious disease, such as smallpox, to rid the house of germs. The most common method of banishing germs was to burn a large amount of an antiseptic, but highly corrosive substance such as sulfur. However, this practice was dangerous to humans and often damaged furniture and household goods.

As scientists researched and tested chemicals, it was discovered that the application of certain chemicals as a method of controlling pests in homes and offices was effective. Chemical research in the 20th century has made possible the use of a variety of substances that are toxic to pests but not harmful to people, pets, or household furnishings, when they are used in the proper quantities.

The use of specially trained pest control technicians arose from this need for precision and knowledge in the application of treatments, and today, the pest control industry does more than $2 billion a year in business.

The Job

The majority of pest control workers are employed as *exterminators* or *pest control technicians*. These workers travel to homes, restaurants, hotels, food stores, warehouses and other places where pests are likely to live and breed. Before starting on their route, they load their truck with pesticides, sprayers, and other necessary equipment, and obtain route slips from company offices showing the customers' names and addresses, services to be performed, and inspection comments. Once at the residence to be serviced, they inspect the premises for rodent droppings, physical damage from insects, and other signs of infestation. They then apply chemical sprays for flies, roaches, beetles, silverfish, and other household insects in cracks in floors and walls, under sinks, and in other places that provide shelter for these pests. Mechanical traps are set for rodents, and poisonous bait is left for them in areas where it will not contaminate food supplies or endanger children or pets.

Sometimes the pest infestation in a house requires the pest control worker to resort to fogging, which involves using a vapor that contains a very small amount of pesticide. This fog penetrates the different places where pests hide. Before fogging, the homeowners must leave for a short while, taking any pets with them. The pest control worker then begins to spray a fine pesticide mist that will not leave deposits on fabrics or flat surfaces. The worker wears a mask or respirator and protective clothing during this procedure. This mist is applied starting in the rear of the house and continuing until the worker exits through the front door. After a certain amount of time, the residents can safely return.

Many commercial establishments have service contracts with an exterminating company that sends workers on a biweekly, monthly, or quarterly basis to make sure the premises remain free of pests. Workers often use a concept known as "integrated pest management" with these customers, which involves advising them on housekeeping and home repair methods to keep pests from returning.

A smaller percentage of pest control workers are *termite exterminators,* and they perform a more extensive and complicated job than other workers in the industry. Termites are particularly destructive pests. Their appetite for wood causes more than $800 million a year in property damage. Termite exterminators treat termites, which live in underground colonies and eat away the foundations and structural members of wooden houses, by laying down a chemical barrier between the termite colony and the structure. This barrier traps the termites either underground, where there is no wood to eat, or in the walls, where they cannot find water. Eventually, the colony dies of either starvation or dehydration. Another method of treating termite infestation involves pumping gaseous pesticides into buildings that have been sealed or covered by tarpaulins.

Termite exterminators must sometimes make structural changes to the buildings they service. Holes may have to be drilled in basement floors to pump chemicals into the soil under the house. To keep termites from returning, exterminators must sometimes raise foundations or replace infested wood. If this alteration work is very extensive, however, the homeowner usually calls in building contractors and carpenters. Once termites have been thoroughly eradicated from a building, they are not likely to return soon. For this reason, termite exterminators work on a single-visit rather than a contract basis. The work of several exterminators may be directed and coordinated by an *extermination supervisor.*

In addition to the above duties, pest control workers must keep records of the dates each account is serviced, the type and strength of pesticides used, and any reported pest problems. They may also be responsible for collecting payment on accounts.

Requirements

High School

The minimum requirement for pest control occupations is a high school diploma. A college degree is not required, although nearly half of all pest controllers have attended college or earned a degree. High school classes such as shop, earth science, math, writing, and chemistry would be beneficial to this profession.

Postsecondary Training

Pest controllers usually begin as apprentices when they learn pesticide safety and use. At this time they also train in one or more of several pest control categories, such as nuisance pest control, wood preservation and treatment, termite control, fumigation, and ornamental and turf control. Training includes approximately 10 hours in the classroom and 60 hours on the job for each specialty. Apprentices have up to one year to prepare for and pass the written examinations, after which they become licensed technicians.

Certification or Licensing

Under the Federal Insecticide, Fungicide, and Rodenticide Act, all pesticide products are classified by the degree of hazard they pose to people and the environment. Therefore, pest control workers must be licensed in many states. Some of these states also require the applicant to pass a written examination. Because many pest control workers have access to residences and businesses, most exterminating companies require that their employees be bonded. This means an employee must be at least 18 years of age and have no criminal record.

Other Requirements

Pest control technicians should be able to use good judgment, and follow oral and written instructions well. These workers should also be very conscientious and responsible, because any mistakes they make applying or handling chemicals could result in serious injury or even death for either themselves or their clients.

Pest control workers should be in good general health and able to lift fairly heavy objects. Because route workers usually make service calls alone, they need a driver's license, a safe driving record, and the ability to work well alone. Manual dexterity and mechanical ability are also important for pest control workers. Termite exterminators will also find knowledge of carpentry valuable.

Exploring

The student who is interested in becoming a pest control worker might want to talk to someone already working in the field to get a good perspective on what the job is like. Students who have held part-time and summer jobs as drivers or helpers on milk, bakery, dry-cleaning, or other routes will find the experience helpful if they plan to enter this field. Also working part-time in the landscaping and lawn products business would be a good experience. An interest in chemistry or, in the case of termite exterminators, in woodworking and carpentry is also an asset. More information regarding this profession can be obtained by contacting your local library or the sources at the end of this article.

Employers

Pest control jobs are available across the country, but most workers are employed in large, high-density population areas. Pest control companies and landscaping and lawn services may employ pest control workers. Some government agencies and large manufacturing or processing companies may hire their own pest control workers as part of their routine maintenance. Some pest control workers operate their own businesses.

Starting Out

Pest control workers usually obtain their jobs through newspaper ads or leads from friends. Job seekers can also apply directly to local pest control firms listed in the Yellow Pages. Owners of firms who use the services of a pest control company may be able to provide job seekers with names of pest control firms. State and local employment offices may have job opportunities with pest control firms.

Advancement

Skilled pest control workers may be promoted to higher-paying jobs, such as *route manager,* responsible for planning out daily or weekly schedules . Those with job experience and sales aptitude may become *pest control salespersons* that contact prospective customers to inform them of the firm's services. They might also become employees of firms that make pesticides or equipment for the industry. Other workers may get jobs as *service managers* and act as liaisons between the company and its customers. Some may advance to owning their own exterminating businesses. Termite exterminators who are skilled at structural work may become carpenters.

Earnings

Salaries vary according to geographic area and company. Beginning technicians can earn between $5 and $6 per hour. According to the *Occupational Outlook Handbook,* the lowest 10 percent of pest controllers earn less than $6.68 an hour. The middle 50 percent earn between $8.80 and $13.02 an hour. The top 10 percent earn over $15.67 an hour. Some technicians receive commission based on a percentage of the service charge to the customer, and others receive a percentage of the route income.

Most pest control companies give their full-time workers regular vacations, health insurance, pension plans, and other benefits.

Work Environment

Most pest control workers are employed in urban areas, where older buildings provide easy access and good shelter for roaches, rats, and other pests. Termite exterminators tend to work in suburbs and small towns, where there are many wood frame buildings. They usually work a 40-hour week, but may work longer hours in the spring and summer when insects and rodents are most active. Sometimes they have to work nights if an establishment such as a restaurant does not want spraying to occur in front of their customers.

Most pest control technicians work alone, driving to each individual client's property. They must often carry equipment and supplies weighing as much as 50 pounds. The job requires them to work both indoors and outdoors, in all kinds of weather, and they usually spend a large amount of time walking and driving. Termite exterminators may have to crawl under buildings and work in dirty or damp cellars. Therefore, people with a strong aversion to dirt, and who are sensitive to unpleasant odors, or who have strong allergies are not well suited to this field. In addition, because the nature of the job requires workers to spend time in pest-infested houses, anyone who is disturbed or frightened by the various bugs or rodents that might be encountered is not a good candidate.

Most of the chemicals used in exterminating are not harmful to humans if handled properly, although some may be injurious if inhaled in large quantities or left on the skin. Pest control workers wear rubber gloves when mixing the pesticides, in addition to other protective clothing. To make certain that workers are safe, some companies routinely take blood samples to test for any residual amounts of the pesticides they use.

Outlook

The demand for pest control workers is expected to grow faster than the average for all occupations through 2008. This growth will be due to increased environmental and health concerns, greater numbers of dual income households, and newer insulation materials that have made certain homes more susceptible to pest infestation. Although steady advances in science are resulting in safer and more effective pesticides, pest control will always be needed, since most vermin breed rapidly and develop an immunity to pesticides over time. The high turnover rate among employees will also provide a certain number of job openings.

Pest control jobs are concentrated in warmer climates. In 1997, more than half of all pest control workers worked in California, Florida, Georgia, North Carolina, Tennessee, and Texas.

For More Information

For information on correspondence courses in pest control, contact:

Department of Entomology, Purdue University
1158 Entomology Hall
West Lafayette, IN 47907
Tel: 765-494-4566
Web: http://www.entm.purdue.edu/

For information on education and careers in the pest control industry, contact:

National Pest Management Association
8100 Oak Street
Dunn Loring, VA 22027
Tel: 703-573-8330
Web: http://www.pestworld.org

Pet Groomers

School Subjects	
Art	
Business	
Health	
Personal Skills	
Artistic	
Helping/teaching	
Work Environment	
Indoors and outdoors	
Primarily one location	
Minimum Education Level	
High school diploma	
Salary Range	
$14,300 to $20,000 to $23,690+	
Certification or Licensing	
Voluntary	
Outlook	
Faster than the average	

Overview

Pet groomers comb, cut, trim, and shape the fur of all types of dogs and cats. They comb out the animal's fur and trim the hair to the proper style for the size and breed. They also trim the animal's nails, bathe it, and dry its hair. In the process, they check for flea or tick infestation and any visible health problems. In order to perform these grooming tasks, the pet groomer must be able to calm the animal down and gain its confidence.

History

As long as dog has been man's best friend, humans have been striving to keep their animal companions healthy and happy. Pets are often considered members of the family and are treated as such. Just as parents take their children to the doctor for vaccinations and to the barber for haircuts, pets are often treated to regular veterinarian visits and grooming services.

An increasingly urban society and higher standards of living can both be considered significant factors in the growing number of professional grooming establishments in this country. City-dwellers who live in small apartments have less space to groom their pets than their farm-dwelling forebears had. Many busy professionals have neither the time nor the inclination to learn the proper techniques and purchase the tools needed for grooming. Additionally, many apartment and condominium buildings have regulations to which pet owners must adhere in order to ensure the safety and comfort of tenants. In compact living quarters, people don't want to encounter smelly pups in the hallway. Also, the rise of multiple-income families and an increased standard of living gives animal aficionados the disposable income to pamper their pets with professional grooming services.

Groomers are also called upon to tend to more exotic pets these days, such as ferrets, birds, and reptiles. New developments in animal grooming include high performance clippers and cutting tools and more humane restraining devices. Current trends toward specialized services include perfuming, powdering, styling, and even massage, aromatherapy, and tattooing for pets!

The Job

Although all dogs and cats benefit from regular grooming, shaggy, longhaired dogs give pet groomers the bulk of their business. Some types of dogs need regular grooming for their standard appearance; among this group are poodles, schnauzers, cocker spaniels, and many types of terriers. Show dogs, or dogs that are shown in competition, are groomed frequently. Before beginning grooming, the dog groomer talks with the owner to find out the style of cut that the dog is to have. The dog groomer also relies on experience to determine how a particular breed of dog is supposed to look.

The dog groomer places the animal on a grooming table. To keep the dog steady during the clipping, a nylon collar or noose, which hangs from an adjustable pole attached to the grooming table, is slipped around its neck. The dog groomer talks to the dog or uses other techniques to keep the animal calm and gain its trust. If the dog doesn't calm down but snaps and bites instead, the groomer may have to muzzle it. If a dog is completely unmanageable, the dog groomer may ask the owner to have the dog tranquilized by a veterinarian before grooming.

After calming the dog, the groomer brushes it and tries to untangle its hair. If the dog's hair is very overgrown or is very shaggy such as an English sheepdog's, the groomer may have to cut away part of its coat with scissors before beginning any real grooming. Brushing the coat is good for both long-haired and shorthaired dogs as brushing removes shedding hair and dead skin. It also neatens the coat so the groomer can tell from the shape and proportions of the dog how to cut its hair in the most attractive way. Hair that is severely matted is actually painful to the animal because the mats pull at the animal's skin. Having these mats removed is necessary to the animal's health and comfort.

Once the dog is brushed, the groomer cuts and shapes the dog's coat with electric clippers. Next, the dog's ears are cleaned and its nails are trimmed. The groomer must take care not to cut the nails too short because they may bleed and cause the dog pain. If the nails do bleed, a special powder is applied to stop the bleeding. The comfort of the animal is an important concern for the groomer.

The dog is then given a bath, sometimes by a worker known as a *dog bather*. The dog is lowered into a stainless steel tub, sprayed with warm water, scrubbed with a special shampoo, and rinsed. This may be repeated several times if the dog is very dirty. The dog groomer has special chemicals that can be used to deodorize a dog that has encountered a skunk or has gone for a swim in foul water. If a dog has fleas or ticks, the dog groomer treats them at this stage by soaking the wet coat with a solution to kill the insects. This toxic solution must be kept out of the dog's eyes, ears, and nose, which may be cleaned more carefully with a sponge or washcloth. A hot oil treatment may also be applied to condition the dog's coat.

The groomer dries the dog after bathing, either with a towel, hand-held electric blower, or in a drier cage with electric blow driers. Poodles and some other types of dogs have their coats fluff-dried, then scissored for the final pattern or style. Poodles, which at one time were the mainstay of the dog grooming business, generally take the longest to groom because of their intricate clipping pattern. Most dogs can be groomed in about 90 minutes, although grooming may take several hours for shaggier breeds whose coats are badly matted and overgrown.

More and more cats, especially longhaired breeds, are now being taken to pet groomers. The procedure for cats is the same as for dogs, although cats are not dipped when bathed. As the dog or cat is groomed, the groomer checks to be sure there are no signs of disease in the animal's eyes, ears, skin, or coat. If there are any abnormalities, such as bald patches or skin lesions, the groomer tells the owner and may recommend that a veterinarian check the animal. The groomer may also give the owner tips on animal hygiene.

Pet owners and those in pet care generally have respect for pet groomers who do a good job and treat animals well. Many people, especially those who raise show dogs, grow to rely on particular pet groomers to do a perfect job each time. Pet groomers can earn satisfaction from taking a shaggy, unkempt animal and transforming it into a beautiful creature. On the other hand, some owners may unfairly blame the groomer if the animal becomes ill while in the groomer's care or for some malady or condition that is not the groomer's fault.

Because they deal with both the pets and their owners, pet groomers can find their work both challenging and rewarding. One owner of a grooming business asserts, "Nothing feels better than developing a relationship with pets and their owners. It's almost like they become an extended part of the family. When working with living animals you accept the responsibility of caring for them to the best of your ability, and the rewards are great. I don't think that can be said of a mechanic or furnace repairman."

Requirements

High School

A high school diploma generally is not required for people working as pet groomers. A diploma or GED certificate, however, can be a great asset to people who would like to advance within their present company or move to other careers in animal care that require more training, such as veterinary technicians. Useful courses include English, business math, general science, anatomy and physiology, health, zoology, psychology, bookkeeping, office management, typing, art, and first aid.

Postsecondary Training

A person interested in pet grooming can be trained for the field in one of three ways: enrolling in a pet grooming school; working in a pet shop or kennel and learning on the job; or reading one of the many books on pet grooming and practicing on his or her own pet.

To enroll in most pet grooming schools, a person must be at least 17 years old and fond of animals. Previous experience in pet grooming can sometimes be applied for course credits. Students study a wide range of topics including the basics of bathing, brushing, and clipping, the care of ears and nails, coat and skin conditions, animal anatomy terminology, and sanitation. They also study customer relations, which is very important for those who plan to operate their own shops. During training, students practice their techniques on actual animals, which people bring in for grooming at a discount rate.

Students can also learn pet grooming while working for a grooming shop, kennel, animal hospital, or veterinarian's office. They usually begin with tasks such as shampooing dogs and cats, and trimming their nails, then gradually work their way up to brushing and basic haircuts. With experience, they may learn more difficult cuts and use these skills to earn more pay or start their own business.

The essentials of pet grooming can also be learned from any of several good books available on grooming. These books contain all the information a person needs to know to start his or her own pet grooming business, including the basic cuts, bathing and handling techniques, and type of equipment needed. Still, many of the finer points of grooming, such as the more complicated cuts and various safety precautions, are best learned while working under an experienced groomer. There still is no substitute for on-the-job training and experience.

Certification or Licensing

Presently, state licensing or certification is not required, and there are no established labor unions for pet groomers. To start a grooming salon or other business, a license is needed from the city or town in which a person plans to practice.

Other Requirements

The primary qualification for a person who wants to work with pets is a love of animals. Animals can sense when someone does not like them or is afraid of them. A person needs certain skills in order to work with nervous, aggressive, or fidgety animals. They must be patient with the animals, able to gain their respect, and enjoy giving the animals a lot of love and attention. Persistence and endurance are also helpful as grooming one animal can take several hours of strenuous work. Groomers should enjoy working with their hands and have good eyesight and manual dexterity to accurately cut a clipping pattern.

Exploring

To find out if they are suited for a job in pet grooming, students should familiarize themselves with animals as much as possible. This can be done in many ways, starting with the proper care of the family pet. Students can also offer to tend to the pets of friends and neighbors to see how well they handle unfamiliar animals. Youth organizations such as the Boy Scouts, Girl Scouts, and 4-H Clubs sponsor projects that give members the chance to raise and care for animals. Students also may do part-time or volunteer work caring for animals at an animal hospital, kennel, pet shop, animal shelter, nature center, or zoo.

Employers

Grooming salons, kennels, pet shops, veterinary practices, animal hospitals, and grooming schools employ pet groomers. The pet business is thriving all over the country, and the opportunities for groomers are expected to increase steadily in the coming years. Although most employers can offer attractive benefits packages, many pet groomers choose to go into business for themselves rather than turn over 40 to 50 percent of their fees to their employers. Graduates of accredited pet grooming schools benefit from the schools' job placement services, which can help students find work in the kind of setting they prefer.

Starting Out

The best ways for most people to gain a thorough knowledge of dog grooming is through hands-on experience and enrollment in an accredited pet grooming course or a pet grooming school. The National Dog Groomers Association of America provides a referral listing of approximately 40 dog grooming schools throughout the United States to persons who send a stamped, self-addressed envelope. Three schools of dog grooming are recognized by the National Association of Trade and Technical Schools: the Pedigree Professional School of Dog Grooming, the New York School of Dog Grooming (three branches), and the Nash Academy of Animal Arts. Many other dog grooming schools advertise in dog and pet magazines. It is important for students to choose an accredited, licensed school in order to increase both their employment opportunities and professional knowledge.

Graduates from dog grooming schools can take advantage of the schools' job placement services. Generally, there are more job openings than qualified groomers to fill them, so new graduates may have several job offers to consider. These schools learn of job openings in all parts of the United States and are usually happy to contact prospective employers and write letters of introduction for graduates.

The National Dog Groomers Association of America also promotes professional identification through membership and certification testing throughout the United States and Canada. The association offers continuing education, accredited workshops, certification testing, seminars, insurance programs, a job placement program, membership directory, and other services and products. Other associations of interest to dog groomers are the Humane Society of the United States and the United Kennel Club. Because dog groomers are concerned with the health and safety of the animals they service, membership in groups that promote and protect animal welfare is very common.

Other sources of job information include the classified ads of daily newspapers and listings in dog and pet magazines. Job leads may be available from private or state employment agencies or from referrals of salon or kennel owners. People looking for work should phone or send letters to prospective employers, inform them of their qualifications, and, if invited, visit their establishments.

Advancement

Pet groomers who work for other people may advance to a more responsible position such as office manager or dog trainer. If dog groomers start their own shops, they may become successful enough to expand or to open branch offices or area franchises. Skilled groomers may want to work for a dog grooming school as an instructor, possibly advancing to a job as a school director, placement officer, or other type of administrator.

The pet industry is booming, so there are many avenues of advancement for groomers who like to work with pets. With more education, a groomer may get a job as a veterinary technician or assistant at a shelter or animal hospital. Those who like to train dogs may open obedience schools, train guide dogs, work with field and hunting dogs, or even train stunt and movie dogs. People can also open their own kennels, breeding and pedigree services, gaming dog businesses, or pet supply distribution firms. Each of these requires specialized knowledge and experience, so additional study, education, and work is often needed.

Earnings

Groomers charge either by the job or the hour. If they are on the staff of a salon or work for another groomer, they get to keep 50 to 60 percent of the fees they charge. For this reason, many groomers branch off to start their own businesses. "I would never want to go back to working for someone else or giving up a commission on my groomings," says one owner-operator of a grooming business.

According to the *O*Net Dictionary of Occupational Titles,* animal groomers can expect to earn $14,300 per year, while the Bureau of Labor Statistics reports that the top 10 percent of workers in the field earned more than $455 per week ($23,690 per year) in 1998. Those who own and operate their own grooming services can earn significantly more, depending on how hard they work, the clientele they service, and the economy of the area in which they work.

Groomers generally buy their own clipping equipment, including barber's shears, brushes, and clippers. A new set of equipment costs around $325; used sets cost less. Groomers employed full time at salons, grooming schools, pet shops, animal hospitals, and kennels often get a full range of benefits, including paid vacations and holidays, medical and dental insurance, and retirement pensions.

Work Environment

Salons, kennels, and pet shops, as well as gaming and breeding services, should be clean and well lighted, with modern equipment and clean surroundings. Establishments that do not meet these standards endanger the health of the animals that are taken there and the owners of these establishments should be reported. Groomers who are self-employed may work out of their homes. Some groomers buy vans and convert them into grooming shops. They drive them to the homes of the pets they work on, which many owners find very convenient. Those who operate these "groommobiles" may work on 30 or 40 dogs a week, and factor their driving time and expenses into their fees.

Groomers usually work a 40-hour week and may have to work evenings or weekends. Those who own their own shops or work out of their homes, like other self-employed people, work very long hours and may have irregular schedules. One groomer points out that, "You can't just decide to call in sick when you have seven dogs scheduled to be groomed that day. We have had midnight emergency calls from clients needing immediate help of one kind or another with their pet." Many groomers/business owners believe that the occasionally hectic schedule of the field is not always a negative aspect, since they take great pride in being able to offer personal service and care to both animals and clients.

Groomers are on their feet much of the day, and their work can get very tiring when they have to lift and restrain large animals. They must wear comfortable clothing that allows for freedom of movement, but they should also be presentable enough to deal with pet owners and other clients.

When working with any sort of animal, a person may encounter bites, scratches, strong odors, fleas, and other insects. They may have to deal with sick or bad-tempered animals. The groomer must regard every animal as a unique individual and treat it with respect. Groomers need to be careful while on the job, especially when handling flea and tick killers, which are toxic to humans as well as the pests.

Outlook

The demand for skilled dog groomers has grown faster than average, and is expected to continue to grow at this rate through 2008. The National Dog Groomers Association of America estimates that more than 30,000 dog groomers are currently employed, and expects that more than 3,000 new groomers will be needed every year during the next decade.

Every year more people are keeping dogs and cats as pets. They are spending more money to pamper their animals, but often don't have enough free time or the inclination to groom their pets themselves. Grooming is not just a luxury for pets, however, because regular attention makes it more likely that any injury or illness will be noticed and treated.

Also, as nontraditional pets become more mainstream, innovative groomers will need to take advantage of new techniques and facilities for bringing animals other than dogs and cats into the pet salon.

For More Information

For information on new grooming products and techniques, as well as workshop and certification test sites and dates, contact the following organizations:

Intergroom
76 Carol Drive
Dedham, MA 02026
Tel: 781-326-3376
Email: intergroom@msn.com
Web: http://www.intergroom.com/

National Dog Groomers Association of America, Inc.
PO Box 101
Clark, PA 16113
Tel: 724-962-2711
Email: ndga@nauticom.net
Web: http://www.nauticom.net/www/ndga

For information on pet grooming schools and certification, contact:

California School of Dog Grooming
655 South Rancho Santa Fe Road
San Marcos, CA 92069
Tel: 800-949-3746
Email: ginny@csdg.net
Web: http://www.csdg.net

New York School of Dog Grooming
248 East 34th Street
New York, NY 10016
Tel: 212-685-3776

Nash Academy of Animal Arts
843 Lane Allen Road
Lexington, KY 40504
Tel: 859-276-5301

For links to additional pet grooming career information, check out the following Web site:

PetGroomer.com
Web: http://www.petgroomer.com

Pet Sitters

	School Subjects
Business Family and consumer science	

	Personal Skills
Following instructions Helping/teaching	

	Work Environment
Indoors and outdoors Primarily multiple locations	

	Minimum Education Level
High school diploma	

	Salary Range
$5,000 to $20,000 to $40,000+	

	Certification or Licensing
Voluntary	

	Outlook
Faster than the average	

Overview

When pet owners are on vacation or working long hours, they hire *pet sitters* to come to their homes and visit their animals. During short, daily visits, pet sitters feed the animals, play with them, clean up after them, give them medications when needed, and let them in and out of the house for exercise. *Dog walkers* may be responsible only for taking their clients' pets out for exercise. Pet sitters may also be available for overnight stays, looking after the houses of clients as well as their pets.

History

Animals have been revered by humans for centuries, as is evidenced by early drawings on the walls of caves and tombs—cats were even considered sacred by the ancient Egyptians. Though these sacred cats may have had their own personal caretakers, it has only been within the last 10 years that pet sitting has evolved into a successful industry and a viable career option. Before groups such as the National Association of Professional Pet Sitters (NAPPS), which formed in the early 1980s, and Pet Sitters International (PSI) were developed, pet sitting was regarded as a way for people with spare time to make a little extra money on the side. Like babysitting, pet sitting attracted primarily teenagers and women; many children's books over the last century have depicted the trials and tribulations of young entrepreneurs in the business of pet sitting and dog walking. Patti Moran, the founder of both NAPPS and PSI, and author of *Pet Sitting for Profit,* is credited with helping pet sitters gain recognition as successful small business owners. Though many people still only pet sit occasionally for neighbors and friends, others are developing long lists of clientele and proving strong competition to kennels and boarding facilities.

The Job

If you live in a big city, you've seen them hit the streets with their packs of dogs. Dragged along by four or five leashes, the pet sitter walks the dogs down the busy sidewalks, allowing the animals their afternoon exercise while the pet owners are stuck in the office. You may not have realized it, but those dog walkers are probably the owners of thriving businesses. Though a hobby for some, pet sitting is for others a demanding career with many responsibilities. Michele Finley is one of these pet sitters, in the Park Slope neighborhood of Brooklyn, New York. "A lot of people seem to think pet sitting is a walk in the park (pun intended)," she says, "and go into it without realizing what it entails (again)."

For those who can't bear to leave their dogs or cats at kennels or boarders while they are away, pet sitters offer peace of mind to the owners, as well as their pets. With a pet sitter, pets can stay in familiar surroundings, as well as avoid the risks of illnesses passed on by other animals. The pets are also assured routine exercise and no disruptions in their diets. Most pet sitters prefer to work only with cats and dogs, but pet sitters are also called upon to care for birds, reptiles, gerbils, fish, and other animals.

With their own set of keys, pet sitters let themselves into the homes of their clients and care for their animals while they're away at work or on vacation. Pet sitters feed the animals, make sure they have water, and give them their medications. They clean up any messes the animals have made and clean litter boxes. They give the animals attention, playing with them, letting them outside, and taking them for walks. Usually, a pet sitter can provide pet owners with a variety of personal pet care services—they may take a pet to the vet, offer grooming, sell pet-related products, and give advice. Some pet sitters take dogs out into the country, to mountain parks, or to lakes, for exercise in wide-open spaces. "You should learn to handle each pet as an individual," Finley advises. "Just because Fluffy likes his ears scratched doesn't mean Spot does."

Pet sitters typically plan one to three visits (of 30 to 60 minutes in length) per day, or they may make arrangements to spend the night. In addition to caring for the animals, pet sitters also look after the houses of their clients. They bring in the newspapers and the mail; they water the plants; they make sure the house is securely locked. Pet sitters generally charge by the hour or per visit. They may also have special pricing for overtime, emergency situations, extra duties, and travel.

Most pet sitters work alone, without employees, no matter how demanding the work. Though this means getting to keep all the money, it also means keeping all the responsibilities. A successful pet sitting service requires a fair amount of business management. Finley works directly with the animals from 10:00 AM until 5:00 or 6:00 PM, with no breaks; upon returning home, she will have five to 10 phone messages from clients. Part of her evening then consists of scheduling and rescheduling appointments, offering advice on feeding, training, and other pet care concerns, and giving referrals for boarders and vets. But despite these hours, and despite having to work holidays, as well as days when she's not feeling well, Finley appreciates many things about the job. "Being with the furries all day is the best," she says. She also likes not having to dress up for work and not having to commute to an office.

Requirements

High School

As a pet sitter, you'll be running your own business all by yourself; therefore you should take high school courses such as accounting, marketing, and office skills. Computer science will help you learn about the software you'll need for managing accounts and scheduling. Join a school business group that will introduce you to business practices and local entrepreneurs.

Science courses such as biology and chemistry, as well as health courses, will give you some good background for developing animal care skills. As a pet sitter, you'll be overseeing the health of the animals, their exercise, and their diets. You'll also be preparing medications and administering eye and ear drops.

As a high school student, you can easily gain hands-on experience as a pet sitter. If you know anyone in your neighborhood with pets, volunteer to care for the animals whenever the owners go on vacation. Once you've got experience and a list of references, you may even be able to start a part-time job for yourself as a pet sitter.

Postsecondary Training

Many pet sitters start their own businesses after having gained experience in other areas of animal care. Vet techs and pet shop workers may promote their animal care skills to develop a clientele for more profitable pet sitting careers. Graduates from a business college may recognize pet sitting as a great way to start a business with little overhead. But neither a vet tech qualification nor a business degree is required to become a successful pet sitter. And the only special training you need to pursue is actual experience. A local pet shop or chapter of the American Society for the Prevention of Cruelty to Animals may offer seminars in various aspects of animal care; Pet Sitters International (PSI) sponsors correspondence programs.

Certification or Licensing

PSI offers accreditation on four levels: Pet Sitting Technician, Advanced Pet Sitting Technician, Master Professional Pet Sitter, and Accredited Pet Sitting Service. Pet sitters receive accreditation upon completing home study courses in such subjects as animal nutrition, office procedures, and management. Because the accreditation program was developed only within the last few years, PSI estimates that less than 10 percent of pet sitters working today are accredited. That number is likely to increase, though there are no plans for any kind of government regulation that would require accreditation. "I really don't think such things are necessary," Finley says about accreditation. "All you need to know can be learned by working for a good sitter and reading pet health and behavioral newsletters."

Though there is no particular pet-sitting license required of pet sitters, insurance protection is important. Liability insurance protects the pet sitter from lawsuits. Pet sitters must also be bonded. Bonding assures the pet owners that if anything is missing from their homes after a pet sitting appointment, they can receive compensation immediately.

Other Requirements

You must love animals and animals must love you. But this love for animals can't be your only motivation—keep in mind that, as a pet sitter, you'll be in business for yourself. You won't have a boss to give you assignments, and you won't have a secretary or bookkeeper to do the paperwork. You also won't have employees to take over on weekends, holidays, and days when you're not feeling well. Though some pet sitters are successful enough to afford assistance, most must handle all the aspects of their businesses by themselves. So, you should be self-motivated, and as dedicated to the management of your business as you are to the animals.

Pet owners are entrusting you with the care of their pets and their homes, so you must be trustworthy and reliable. You should also be organized and prepared for emergency situations. And not only must you be patient with the pets and their owners, but also with the development of your business: it will take a few years to build up a good list of clients.

As a pet sitter, you must also be ready for the dirty work—you'll be cleaning litter boxes and animal messes within the house. On dog walks, you'll be picking up after them on the street. You may be giving animals medications. You'll also be cleaning aquariums and bird cages.

"Work for an established pet sitter to see how you like it," Finley advises. "It's a very physically demanding job and not many can stand it for long on a full-time basis." Pet sitting isn't for those who just want a nine-to-five desk job. Your day will be spent moving from house to house, taking animals into backyards, and walking dogs around the neighborhoods. Though you may be able to develop a set schedule for yourself, you really will have to arrange your work hours around the hours of your clients. Some pet sitters start in the early morning hours, while others only work afternoons or evenings. To stay in business, a pet sitter must be prepared to work weekends, holidays, and long hours in the summertime.

Exploring

There are many books, newsletters, and magazines devoted to pet care. *Pet Sitting for Profit,* by Patti Moran, and *The Professional Pet Sitter,* by Lori and Scott Mangold, are a few of the books that can offer insight into pet sitting as a career. Magazines such as *Dog Fancy* and *Cat Fancy* can also teach you about the requirements of animal care. And there are any number of books discussing the ins and outs of small business ownership.

Try pet sitting for a neighbor or family member to get a sense of the responsibilities of the job. Some pet sitters hire assistants on an independent contractor basis; contact an area pet sitter listed in the phone book or with one of the professional organizations, and see if you can "hire on" for a day or two. Not only will you learn firsthand the duties of a pet sitter, but you'll also see how the business is run.

Employers

Nearly all pet sitters are self-employed, although a few may work for other successful pet sitters who have built up a large enough clientele to require help. It takes most pet sitters an appreciable period of time to build up a business substantial enough to make a living without other means of income. However, the outlook for this field is excellent and start-up costs are minimal, making it a good choice for animal lovers who want to work for themselves. For those who have good business sense and a great deal of ambition, the potential for success is good.

Starting Out

You're not likely to find job listings under "pet sitter" in the newspaper. Most pet sitters schedule all their work themselves. However, you may find ads in the classifieds or in weekly community papers, from pet owners looking to hire pet sitters. Some people who become pet sitters have backgrounds in animal care—they may have worked for vets, breeders, or pet shops. These people enter the business with a client list already in hand, having made contacts with many pet owners. But, if you're just starting out in animal care, you need to develop a list of references. This may mean volunteering your time to friends and neighbors, or working very cheaply. If you're willing to actually stay in the house while the pet owners are on vacation, you should be able to find plenty of pet sitting opportunities in the summertime. Post your name, phone number, and availability on the bulletin boards of grocery stores, colleges, and coffee shops around town. Once you've developed a list of references, and have made connections with pet owners, you can start expanding, and increasing your profits.

Advancement

Your advancement will be a result of your own hard work; the more time you dedicate to your business, the bigger the business will become. The success of any small business can be very unpredictable. For some, a business can build very quickly, for others it may take years. Some pet sitters start out part-time, perhaps even volunteering, then may find themselves with enough business to quit their full-time jobs and devote themselves entirely to pet sitting. Once your business takes off, you may be able to afford an assistant, or an entire staff. Some pet sitters even have franchises across the country. You may even choose to develop your business into a much larger operation, such as a dog day care facility.

Earnings

Pet sitters set their own prices, charging by the visit, the hour, or the week. They may also charge consultation fees, and additional fees on holidays. They may have special pricing plans in place, such as for emergency situations or for administering medications. Depending on the kinds of animals (sometimes pet sitters charge less to care for cats than dogs), pet sitters generally charge between $8 and $15 a visit (with a visit lasting between 30 and 60 minutes). Pet Sitters International conducted a recent salary survey and discovered that the range was too great to determine a median. Some very successful pet sitters have annual salaries of over $100,000, while others only make $5,000 a year. Though a pet sitter can make a good profit in any area of the country, a bigger city will offer more clients. Pet sitters in their first five years of business are unlikely to make more than $10,000 a year; pet sitters who have had businesses for eight years or more may make more than $40,000 a year.

Work Environment

Some pet sitters prefer to work close to their homes; Finley only walks dogs in her Brooklyn neighborhood. In a smaller town, however, pet sitters have to do a fair amount of driving from place to place. Depending on the needs of the animals, the pet sitter will let the pets outside for play and exercise.

Although filling food and water bowls and performing other chores within the house is generally peaceful work, walking dogs on busy city sidewalks can be stressful. And in the wintertime, you'll spend a fair amount of time out in the inclement weather. "Icy streets are murder," Finley says. "And I don't like dealing with people who hate dogs and are always yelling to get the dog away from them."

Though you'll have some initial interaction with pet owners when getting house keys, taking down phone numbers, and meeting the pets and learning about their needs, most of your work will be alone with the animals. But you won't be totally isolated; if dog walking in the city, you'll meet other dog owners and other people in the neighborhood.

Outlook

Pet sitting as a small business is expected to skyrocket in the coming years. Most pet sitters charge fees comparable to kennels and boarders, but some charge less. And many pet owners prefer to leave their pets in the house, rather than take the pets to unfamiliar locations. This has made pet sitting a desirable and cost-effective alternative to other pet care situations. Pet sitters have been successful in cities both large and small. In the last few years, pet sitting has been featured in the *Wall Street Journal* and other national publications; last year, *Woman's Day* magazine listed pet sitting as one of the top-grossing businesses for women. Pet Sitters International has grown 500 percent in the last four years.

Because a pet sitting business requires little money to start up, many more people may enter the business hoping to make a tidy profit. This could lead to heavier competition; it could also hurt the reputation of pet sitting if too many irresponsible and unprepared people run bad businesses. But if pet owners remain cautious when hiring pet sitters, the unreliable workers will have trouble maintaining clients.

For More Information

For career and small business information, as well as general information about pet sitting, contact the following organizations:

American Society for the Prevention of Cruelty to Animals
424 East 92nd Street
New York, NY 10128
Tel: 212-876-7700
Web: http://www.aspca.org/

National Association of Professional Pet Sitters
6 State Road, Suite 113
Mechanicsburg, PA 17050
Tel: 717-691-5565
Email: nappsmail@aol.com
Web: http://www.petsitters.org/

Pet Sitters International
418 East King Street
King, NC 27021-9163
Tel: 336-983-9222
Email: info@petsit.com
Web: http://www.petsit.com

Security Consultants and Technicians

School Subjects
Business
Psychology

Personal Skills
Communication/ideas
Mechanical/manipulative

Work Environment
Indoors and outdoors
One location with some travel

Minimum Education Level
Bachelor's degree
(security consultants)
High school diploma
(security technicians)

Salary Range
$11,970 to $26,640 to $100,000+

Certification or Licensing
Recommended

Outlook
Faster than the average

Overview

Security consultants and technicians are responsible for protecting public and private property against theft, fire, vandalism, illegal entry, and acts of violence. They may work for commercial or government organizations or private individuals. Over one million security workers are employed in the United States.

History

People have been concerned with protecting valuable possessions since they began accumulating goods. At first, most security plans were rather simple. In earliest times, members of extended families or several families would band together to watch food, clothing, livestock, and other valuables. As personal wealth grew, the wealthier members of a society would often assign some of their servants to protect their property and families from theft and violence. Soldiers often filled this function as well. During the Middle Ages, many towns and villages hired guards to patrol the streets at night as protection against fire, theft, and hostile intrusion. Night watchmen continued to play an important role in the security of many towns and cities until well into the 19th century.

The first public police forces were organized in about the middle of the 19th century. These were largely limited to cities, however, and the need for protection and safety of goods and property led many to supplement police forces with private security forces. In the United States, ranchers and others hired armed guards to protect their property. Soon, people began to specialize in offering comprehensive security and detective services. Allan Pinkerton was one of the first such security agents. In 1861, Pinkerton was hired to guard President-elect Abraham Lincoln on his way to his inauguration.

As police forces at local, state, and federal levels were established across the country, night watchmen and other security personnel continued to play an important role in protecting the goods and property of private businesses. The growth of industry created a need for people to patrol factories and warehouses. Many companies hired private security forces to guard factories during strikes. Banks, department stores, and museums employed security guards to guard against theft and vandalism. Other security personnel began to specialize in designing security systems—with considerations including the types of safes and alarms to be used and the stationing of security guards—to protect both public and private facilities. Government and public facilities, such as ammunition dumps, nuclear power facilities, dams, and oil pipelines also needed security systems and guards to protect them.

Security systems have grown increasingly sophisticated with the introduction of technologies such as cameras, closed-circuit television, video, and computers. The security guard continues to play an important role in the protection of people and property. The increasing use of computers has aided the guard or security technician by protecting electronic data and transmissions. The increasing number of terrorist threats has also led to the more frequent use of personal security services. Today, commercial security services is one of the fastest growing fields of employment.

The Job

A security consultant is engaged in protective service work. Anywhere that valuable property or information is present or people are at risk, a security consultant may be called in to devise and implement security plans that offer protection. Security consultants may work for a variety of clients, including large stores, art museums, factories, laboratories, data processing centers, and political candidates. They are involved in preventing theft, vandalism, fraud, kidnapping, and other crimes. Specific job responsibilities depend on the type and size of the client's company and the scope of the security system required.

Security consultants always work closely with company officials or other appropriate individuals in the development of a comprehensive security program that will fit the needs of individual clients. After discussing goals and objectives with the relevant company executives, consultants study and analyze the physical conditions and internal operations of a client's operation. They learn much by simply observing day-to-day operations.

The size of the security budget also influences the type of equipment ordered and methods used. For example, a large factory that produces military hardware may fence off its property and place electric eyes around the perimeter of the fence. They may also install perimeter alarms and use passkeys to limit access to restricted areas. A smaller company may use only entry-control mechanisms in specified areas. The consultant may recommend sophisticated technology, such as closed circuit surveillance or ultrasonic motion detectors, alone or in addition to security personnel. Usually, a combination of electronic and human resources is used.

Security consultants not only devise plans to protect equipment but also recommend procedures on safeguarding and possibly destroying classified material. Increasingly, consultants are being called on to develop strategies to safeguard data processing equipment. They may have to develop measures to safeguard transmission lines against unwanted or unauthorized interceptions.

Once a security plan has been developed, the consultant oversees the installation of the equipment, ensures that it is working properly, and checks frequently with the client to ensure that the client is satisfied. In the case of a crime against the facility, a consultant investigates the nature of the crime (often in conjunction with police or other investigators) and then modifies the security system to safeguard against similar crimes in the future.

Many consultants work for security firms that have several types of clients, such as manufacturing and telecommunications plants and facilities. Consultants may handle a variety of clients or work exclusively in a particular area. For example, one security consultant may be assigned to handle the protection of nuclear power plants and another to handle data processing companies.

Security consultants may be called on to safeguard famous individuals or persons in certain positions from kidnapping or other type of harm. They provide security services to officers of large companies, media personalities, and others who want their safety and privacy protected. These consultants, like bodyguards, plan and review client travel itineraries and usually accompany the client on trips, checking accommodations and appointment locations along the way. They often check the backgrounds of people who will interact with the client, especially those who see the client infrequently.

Security consultants are sometimes called in for special events, such as sporting events and political rallies, when there is no specific fear of danger but rather a need for overall coordination of a large security operation. The consultants oversee security preparation—such as the stationing of appropriate personnel at all points of entry and exit—and then direct specific responses to any security problems.

Security officers develop and implement security plans for companies that manufacture or process material for the federal government. They ensure that their clients' security policies comply with federal regulations in such categories as the storing and handling of classified documents and restricting access to authorized personnel only.

Security guards have various titles, depending on the type of work they do and the setting in which they work. They may be referred to as *patrollers, merchant patrollers, bouncers* (people who eject unruly people from places of entertainment), *golf-course rangers* (who patrol golf courses), or *gate tenders* (who work at security checkpoints). They may work as *airline security representatives* in airports or as armored-car guards and drivers.

Many security guards are employed during normal working hours in public and commercial buildings and other areas with a good deal of pedestrian traffic and public contact. Others patrol buildings and grounds outside normal working hours, such as at night and on weekends. Guards usually wear uniforms and may carry a nightstick. Guards who work in situations where they may be called upon to apprehend criminal intruders are usually armed. They may also carry a flashlight, a whistle, a two-way radio, and a watch clock, which is used to record the time at which they reach various checkpoints.

Guards in public buildings may be assigned to a certain post or they may patrol an area. In museums, art galleries, and other public buildings, guards answer visitors' questions and give them directions; they also enforce rules against smoking, touching art objects, and so forth. In commercial buildings, guards may sign people in and out after hours and inspect packages being carried out of the building. *Bank guards* observe customers carefully for any sign of suspicious behavior that may signal a possible robbery attempt. In department stores, security guards often work with undercover detectives to watch for theft by customers or store employees. Guards at large public gatherings such as sporting events and conventions keep traffic moving, direct people to their seats, and eject unruly spectators. Guards employed at airports limit access to boarding areas to passengers only. They make sure people entering passenger areas have valid tickets and observe passengers and their baggage as they pass through X-ray machines and metal detection equipment.

After-hours guards are usually employed at industrial plants, defense installations, construction sites, and facilities such as docks and railroad yards. They make regular rounds on foot or in motorized vehicles. They make sure no unauthorized persons are on the premises, that doors and windows are secure, and that no property is missing. They may be equipped with walkie-talkies to report in to a guard station. Sometimes guards perform custodial duties, such as turning on lights and setting thermostatic controls.

In a large organization, a security officer is often in charge of the guard force; in a small organization, a single worker may be responsible for all security measures. As more businesses purchase electronic security systems to protect their properties, more guards are being assigned to stations where they monitor perimeter security, communications, and other systems. In many cases, these guards maintain radio contact with other guards patrolling on foot or in motor vehicles. Some guards use computers to store information on matters relevant to security such as visitors or suspicious occurrences during their time on duty.

Security technicians work for government agencies or for private companies hired by government agencies. Their task is usually to guard secret or restricted installations. They spend much of their time patrolling areas, by foot, on horseback, or in automobiles or aircraft. They may monitor activities in an area through the use of cameras. Their assignments usually include detecting and preventing unauthorized activities, searching for explosive devices, standing watch during secret and hazardous experiments, and performing other routine police duties within government installations.

Security technicians are usually armed and may be required to use their weapons or other kinds of physical force to prevent some kinds of activities. They are usually not, however, required to remove explosive devices from an installation. When they find such devices, they notify a bomb disposal unit, which is responsible for removing and then defusing or detonating the device.

Requirements

High School

A high school diploma is preferred for security guards and required for security consultants, who should also go on to obtain a college degree. Security technicians are required to be high school graduates. In addition, they should expect to receive from three to six months of specialized training in security procedures and technology. If you would like to be a security technician, while in high school you should take mathematics courses to ensure that you can perform basic arithmetic operations with different units of measure, compute ratios, rates, and percentages, and interpret charts and graphs.

You should take English courses to develop your reading and writing skills. You should be able to read manuals, memos, textbooks, and other instructional materials and write reports with correct spelling, grammar, and punctuation. You should also be able to speak to small groups with poise and confidence.

Postsecondary Training

Most companies prefer to hire security consultants who have at least a college degree. An undergraduate or associate's degree in criminal justice, business administration, or related field is best. Coursework should be broad and include business management, communications, computer courses, sociology, and statistics. As the security consulting field becomes more competitive, many consultants choose to get a master's in business administration (MBA) or other graduate degree.

Although there are no specific educational or professional requirements, many security consultants have had previous experience with police work or other forms of crime prevention. It is helpful if a person develops an expertise in a specific area. For example, if you want to work devising plans securing data processing equipment, it is helpful to have previous experience working with computers.

Certification or Licensing

Many security consultants are certified by the Certified Protection Professionals. To be eligible for certification, a consultant must pass a written test and have 10 years work and educational experience in the security profession. Information on certification is available from the American Society for Industrial Security, a professional organization to which many security consultants belong.

Virtually every state has licensing or registration requirements for security guards who work for contract security agencies. Registration generally requires that a person newly hired as a guard be reported to the licensing authorities, usually the state police department or special state licensing commission. To be granted a license, individuals generally must be 18 years of age, have no convictions for perjury or acts of violence, pass a background investigation, and complete classroom training on a variety of subjects, including property rights, emergency procedures, and capture of suspected criminals.

Other Requirements

For security guards, general good health (especially vision and hearing), alertness, emotional stability, and the ability to follow directions are important characteristics. Military service and experience in local or state police departments are assets. Prospective guards should have clean police records. Some employers require applicants to take a polygraph examination or a written test that indicates honesty, attitudes, and other personal qualities. Most employers require applicants and experienced workers to submit to drug screening tests as a condition of employment.

For some hazardous or physically demanding jobs, guards must be under a certain age and meet height and weight standards. For top-level security positions in facilities such as nuclear power plants or vulnerable information centers, guards may be required to complete a special training course. They may also need to fulfill certain relevant academic requirements.

Guards employed by the federal government must be U.S. armed forces veterans, have some previous experience as guards, and pass a written examination. Many positions require experience with firearms. In many situations, guards must be bonded.

Security technicians need good eyesight and should be in good physical shape, able to lift at least 50 pounds, climb ladders, stairs, poles, and ropes, and maintain their balance on narrow, slippery, or moving surfaces. They should be able to stoop, crawl, crouch, and kneel with ease.

Exploring

Part-time or summer employment as a clerk with a security firm is an excellent way to gain insight into the skills and temperament needed to become a security consultant. Discussions with professional security consultants are another way of exploring career opportunities in this field. You may find it helpful to join a safety patrol at school.

If you are interested in a particular area of security consulting, such as data processing, for example, you can join a club or association to learn more about the field. This is a good way to make professional contacts.

Opportunities for part-time or summer work as security guards are not generally available to high school students. You may, however, work as a lifeguard, on a safety patrol, and as a school hallway monitor, which can provide helpful experience.

Employers

Security services is one of the largest employment fields in the United States. Over one million persons are employed as security guards in the United States. Industrial security firms and guard agencies, also called contract security firms, employ over 60 percent of all guards, while the remainder are in-house guards employed by various establishments.

Starting Out

People interested in careers in security services generally apply directly to security companies. Some jobs may be available through state or private employment services. People interested in security technician positions should apply directly to government agencies.

Beginning security personnel receive varied amounts of training. Training requirements are generally increasing as modern, highly sophisticated security systems become more common. Many employers give newly hired security guards instruction before they start the job and also provide several weeks of on-the-job training. Guards receive training in protection, public relations, report writing, crisis deterrence, first aid, and drug control.

Those employed at establishments that place a heavy emphasis on security usually receive extensive formal training. For example, guards at nuclear power plants may undergo several months of training before being placed on duty under close supervision. Guards may be taught to use firearms, administer first aid, operate alarm systems and electronic security equipment, handle emergencies, and spot and deal with security problems.

Many of the less strenuous guard positions are filled by older people who are retired police officers or armed forces veterans. Because of the odd hours required for many positions, this occupation appeals to many people seeking part-time work or second jobs.

Most entry-level positions for security consultants are filled by those with a bachelor's or associate's degree in criminal justice, business administration, or a related field. Those with a high school diploma and some experience in the field may find work with a security consulting firm, although they usually begin as security guards and become consultants only after further training.

Because many consulting firms have their own techniques and procedures, most require entry-level personnel to complete an on-the-job training program, during the course of which company policy is introduced.

Advancement

In most cases, security guards receive periodic salary increases, and guards employed by larger security companies or as part of a military-style guard force may increase their responsibilities or move up in rank. A guard with outstanding ability, especially with some college education, may move up to the position of *chief guard*—gaining responsibility for the supervision and training of an entire guard force in an industrial plant or a department store—or become director of security services for a business or commercial building. A few guards with management skills open their own contract security guard agencies; other guards become licensed private detectives. Experienced guards may become *bodyguards,* protecting political figures, executives, and celebrities, or choose to enter a police department or other law enforcement agency. Additional training may lead to a career as a *corrections officer,* responsible for individuals who have been arrested and are awaiting trial or are sentenced to serve time in jail.

Increased training and experience with a variety of security and surveillance systems may lead security guards into higher-paying security consultant careers. Security consultants with experience may advance to management positions or they may start their own private consulting firms. Instruction and training of security personnel is another advancement opportunity for security guards, consultants, and technicians.

Earnings

Earnings for security consultants vary greatly depending on the consultant's training and experience. Entry-level consultants with bachelor's degrees commonly start at $26,000 to $32,000 per year. Consultants with graduate degrees begin at $34,000 to $41,000 per year, and experienced consultants may earn $50,000 to $100,000 per year or more. Many consultants work on a per-project basis, with rates of up to $75 per hour.

Average starting salaries for security guards and technicians vary according to their level of training and experience, and the location where they work. Median annual earnings for security technicians in 1998 were $16,240 in 1998, according to the U.S. Department of Labor. Experienced security guards average as high as $26,640 per year, with those employed in manufacturing facilities receiving the highest wages.

Entry-level guards working for contract agencies may receive little more than the minimum wage, however. In-house guards generally earn higher wages and have greater job security and better advancement potential.

Security guards and technicians employed by federal government agencies earned starting salaries of $16,400 or $18,400 per year in 1999, and they average $26,300 per year with experience. The location of the work also affects earnings, with higher pay in locations with a higher cost of living. Government employees typically enjoy good job security and generous benefits. Benefits for positions with private companies vary significantly.

Work Environment

Consultants usually divide their time between their offices and a client's business. Much time is spent analyzing various security apparatuses and developing security proposals. The consultant talks with a variety of employees at a client's company, including the top officials, and discusses alternatives with other people at the consulting firm. A consultant makes a security proposal presentation to the client and then works with the client on any modifications. Consultants must be sensitive to budget issues and develop security systems that their clients can afford.

Consultants may specialize in one type of security work (nuclear power plants, for example) or work for a variety of large and small clients, such as museums, data processing companies, and banks. Although there may be a lot of travel and some work may require outdoor activity, there will most likely be no strenuous work. A consultant may oversee the implementation of a large security system but is not involved in the actual installation process. A consultant may have to confront suspicious people but is not expected to do the work of a police officer.

Security guards and technicians may work indoors or outdoors. In high-crime areas and industries vulnerable to theft and vandalism, there may be considerable physical danger. Guards who work in museums, department stores, and other buildings and facilities remain on their feet for long periods of time, either standing still or walking while on patrol. Guards assigned to reception areas or security control rooms may remain at their desks for the entire shift. Much of their work is routine and may be tedious at times, yet guards must remain constantly alert during their shift. Guards who work with the public, especially at sporting events and concerts, may have to confront unruly and sometimes hostile people. Bouncers often confront intoxicated people and are frequently called upon to intervene in physical altercations.

Many companies employ guards around the clock in three shifts, including weekends and holidays, and assign workers to these shifts on a rotating basis. The same is true for security technicians guarding government facilities and installations. Those with less seniority will likely have the most erratic schedules. Many guards work alone for an entire shift, usually lasting eight hours. Lunches and other meals are often taken on the job, so that constant vigilance is maintained.

Outlook

Employment for guards and other security personnel is expected to increase faster than the average through 2008, as crime rates rise with the overall population growth. The highest U.S. Department of Labor estimates call for more than 1.25 million guards to be employed by 2008. Many job openings will be created as a result of the high turnover of workers in this field.

A factor adding to this demand is the trend for private security firms to perform duties previously handled by police officers, such as courtroom security and crowd control in airports. Private security companies employ security technicians to guard many government sites, such as nuclear testing facilities. Private companies also operate many training facilities for government security technicians and guards, as well as providing police services for some communities.

For More Information

For information on certification procedures, contact:

American Society for Industrial Security
1625 Prince Street
Alexandria, VA 22314-2818
Tel: 703-519-6200
Email: asis@asisonline.org
Web: http://www.asisonline.org/

For information on union membership, contact the following organizations:

International Security Officers' Police and Guard Union
321 86th Street
Brooklyn, NY 11209
Tel: 718-836-3508

International Union of Security Officers
2404 Merced Street
San Leandro, CA 94577
Tel: 510-895-9905

Swimming Pool Servicers

Chemistry Technical/shop	School Subjects
Following instructions Technical/scientific	Personal Skills
Indoors and outdoors Primarily multiple locations	Work Environment
High school diploma	Minimum Education Level
$20,000 to $40,000 to $50,000+	Salary Range
Voluntary	Certification or Licensing
About as fast as the average	Outlook

Overview

Swimming pool servicers clean, adjust, and perform minor repairs on swimming pools, hot tubs, and their auxiliary equipment. There are millions of pools across the country in hotels, parks, apartment complexes, health clubs, and other public areas. These public pools are required by law to be regularly serviced by trained technicians. In addition, the number of homeowners with personal pools is increasing, and these private pools also need professional servicing.

History

Swimming for enjoyment and physical activity is as old as walking and running. Swimming pools date back to the bathhouses in the palaces of ancient Greece. These bathhouses were elaborate spas, complete with steam rooms, saunas, and large pools. But swimming was a popular pastime even among those who didn't have access to bathhouses; many swam in the rivers, oceans, and the lakes of the world. The plagues of medieval Europe made people cautious about swimming in unclean waters, but soon swimming regained popularity. Swimmers swam with their heads above water in a style developed when people were still afraid of water contamination. This swimming style changed in the mid-1800s when American Indians introduced an early version of the modern "crawl." Swimming in natural spring waters was even recommended as a health benefit, inspiring hospitals and spas to develop around hot springs.

The first modern Olympics held in Athens featured swimming as one of the nine competitions. Swimming as both a sport and a pastime has continued to develop along with the technology of pool maintenance. By the 1960s, the National Swimming Pool Foundation had evolved to support research in pool safety and the education of pool operators.

The Job

Swimming pool servicers travel a regularly scheduled route, visiting several pools a day. They are responsible for keeping pools clean and equipment operating properly. In general, a pool that receives routine maintenance develops fewer problems.

Mark Randall owns a pool service business in Malibu, California. "My tools range from a tile brush to a state of the art computer and printer," he says. Randall has two employees, so his day usually starts with phone calls to his crew and customers. "Then I go out and clean a few of the more difficult accounts," he says.

Cleaning is one of the regular duties of pool servicers. Leaves and other debris need to be scooped off the surface of the water with a net on a long pole. To clean beneath the surface, servicers use a special vacuum cleaner on the pool floor and walls. They scrub pool walls, tiles, and gutters around the pool's edge with stainless steel or nylon brushes to remove layers of grit and scum that collect at the water line. They also hose down the pool deck and unclog the strainers that cover the drains.

After cleaning the pool and its surroundings, servicers test the bacterial content and pH balance (a measure of acidity and alkalinity) of the water. While the tests are simple and take only a few minutes, they are very important. A sample of the pool water is collected in a jar and a few drops of a testing chemical are added to the water. This chemical causes the water to change colors, indicating the water's chemical balance. Swimming pool servicers use these results to determine the amount of chlorine and other chemicals that should be added to make the water safe. The chemicals often used, which include potassium iodide, hydrochloric acid, sodium carbonate, chlorine, and others, are poured directly into the pool or added through a feeder device in the circulation system. These chemicals, when properly regulated, kill bacteria and algae that grow in water. However, high levels of chemicals can cause eye or skin irritation. As a result, pool servicers must wear gloves and use caution when working. Because the chemical makeup of every pool is different and can change daily or even hourly, servicers keep accurate records of the levels of chemicals added to the pool during their visit. Pool owners or managers take up the responsibility of testing the water between visits from the servicer. Home pools usually have their water tested a few times a week, but large public pools are tested hourly.

Swimming pool servicers also inspect and perform routine maintenance on pool equipment, such as circulation pumps, filters, and heaters. In order to clean a filter, servicers force water backwards through it to dislodge any debris that has accumulated. They make sure there are no leaks in pipes, gaskets, connections, or other parts. If a drain or pipe is clogged, servicers use a steel snake, plunger, or other plumbing tool to clear it. They also adjust thermostats, pressure gauges, and other controls to make the pool water comfortable. Minor repairs to machinery, such as fixing or replacing small components, may be necessary. When major repairs are needed, servicers first inform the pool owner before making any repairs.

"An accomplished pool tech," Randall says, "can do a pool in about 20 minutes. Most pool techs would do this 10 to 20 times a day."

Another major task for swimming pool servicers in most regions of the country is closing outdoor pools for the winter. In the fall, servicers drain the water out of the pool and its auxiliary equipment. Openings into the pool are plugged, and all pool gear, such as diving boards, ladders, and pumps, is removed, inspected, and stored. The pool is covered with a tarpaulin and tied or weighted in place. In warmer climates where water does not freeze, pools are usually kept full and treated with special chemicals through the winter.

Extra work is also required when a pool is re-opened in the spring. After the pool is uncovered and the tank and pool deck are swept clean, swimming pool servicers inspect for cracks, leaks, loose tiles, and broken lamps. They repair all minor problems and make recommendations to the owner about any major work they feel is necessary, such as painting the interior of the pool. Equipment removed in the fall, such as ladders and diving boards, is cleaned and installed. Servicers test water circulation and heating systems to make sure they are operating properly, and then fill the pool with water. Once filled, the pool water is tested and the appropriate chemicals are added to make it safe for swimming.

For every job, servicers keep careful records of the maintenance work they have done so they can inform the company and the customer.

Requirements

High School

Take science courses such as chemistry and biology to gain understanding of the chemicals used in testing pool water. Shop courses with lessons in electrical wiring and motors will help to develop skills for repairing and servicing machines and equipment. Bookkeeping and accounting courses are also helpful to learn how to keep financial and tax records. You should also learn about spreadsheet and database software programs because you will probably be using computers to maintain files on profits and expenses, customers, equipment, and employees. Finally, serving as an assistant on a swim team can teach you firsthand about the requirements of maintaining a regulation pool.

Postsecondary Training

You can gain most of the technical training that you will need for this career on the job. By working with another trained professional, you'll learn the basics of pool maintenance within a few months. However, if you are considering running your own business, prepare yourself further by enrolling in college courses in sales, math, accounting, and small business management.

Mark Randall has had college and technical training in various fields and has worked as a mechanic, data analyst, and prop builder for a movie studio. "I had no idea I would end up in the pool business," he says. "Luckily, my background was actually very good training for my current business." He recommends that people interested in pool maintenance take advanced courses in electrical applications, electronics, plumbing, and hydraulics.

Certification and Licensing

Randall believes that certification and licensing are very important to running a professional outfit. He is certified by the health department, has a business license, and belongs to the Independent Pool and Spa Service Organization. Certification is available from the National Swimming Pool Foundation, the National Spa and Pool Institute, and by service franchisers. Certification programs consist of a set number of classroom hours and a written exam. While not a requirement, certification does indicate that you've reached a certain level of expertise and skill and can help you promote your business.

Other Requirements

Because servicers often work alone with minimum supervision, it is important that you have self-discipline and a responsible attitude. Inner drive and ambition will determine the success of your business as you work to attract new clients.

"Persistence is probably the most important quality," Randall says. He also emphasizes a strong work ethic and good communication skills. You'll also need to keep up with the technology of swimming pool maintenance to stay knowledgeable about new equipment and services available to your clients.

Exploring

A summer or part-time job with a school, park district, community center, or local health club can provide you with opportunities to learn more about servicing swimming pools. Hotels, motels, apartment buildings, and condominium complexes also frequently have pools and may hire summer or part-time workers to service them. Such a job could offer firsthand insight into the duties of swimming pool servicers, as well as help in obtaining full-time employment with a pool maintenance company later.

Aqua Magazine is a good source of technical information concerning pool service. Contact the magazine for a sample issue, or visit their Web site (http://www.aquamagazine.com) to read from a selection of online articles.

Employers

A majority of swimming pool servicers are self-employed. With close to 7 million residential swimming pools in the country, pool service owners can find clients in practically every neighborhood. In addition to servicing residential pools, workers service the pools of motels, apartment complexes, and public parks.

Some servicers choose to work with a franchise service company. These franchisers often offer training and usually provide an established client base.

Starting Out

Once servicers have the training and the money to invest in equipment, they work on pursuing clients. This may involve promoting their business through advertising, flyers, and word of mouth. They may be able to get referrals from local pool and spa construction companies.

"I started out riding with a friend who worked for a large pool service company," Mark Randall says, "and I learned as much as I could. After that, I found a small route for sale." Mark borrowed money from the bank to buy the established route of customers, then used his training to start servicing pools. "It was sink or swim, pardon the pun," he says. "But I worked very hard the first couple of years and have been fairly successful."

Advancement

Advancement is usually shown through a growth in business. More area pool construction, positive feedback from customers, and some years in the business will attract more clients and more routes to service. If a business does really well, swimming pool servicers may choose to hire additional employees to do most of the service work, allowing more time to focus on office work and administrative details. Servicers may also expand their business to include the sale of pools, spas, and maintenance equipment.

After many years in the business, Randall is debating his next career move. "I'm toying with the idea of getting a contractor's license," he says, "and building pools."

Earnings

The amount of money swimming pool servicers make depends upon the region of the country in which they work (which determines the length of the swimming season), services provided by the business, and levels of experience. Experts in the business estimate that an experienced pool service owner can average $40,000 to $50,000 a year. Beginning servicers just starting to build a clientele or those that work in an area of the country that allows for only a few months of swimming may earn less than $20,000 a year.

Work Environment

Swimming pool servicers generally work alone and sometimes have little client contact. Most of the work is not particularly strenuous, though kneeling, bending, and carrying equipment from your van to the pool is necessary. Servicers work both indoors and outdoors and usually work in pleasant weather. They must handle chemicals, requiring the use of protective gloves and possibly a breathing mask to guard against fumes.

Pool servicing can be an excellent job for those who enjoy spending time outside. "I find cleaning pools to be kind of relaxing," Mark Randall says, "and a good time to enjoy my surroundings. Some people find it boring and monotonous. I guess you just need a good perspective."

Outlook

According to the National Spa and Pool Institute, pool sales are increasing nationwide. In 1993, there were 2.9 million inground pools and 2.1 million above ground pools. By 1998, those numbers rose to 3.8 million and 3.3 million, respectively. Industry experts attribute this growth to increasing wealth among homeowners, a growing desire to enhance and alter existing homes, and a general rise in the standard of living.

With the growing number of pools, the demand for professionals trained to maintain and repair them will be strong. In addition, with more homeowners installing personal pools, there is growing concern for pool safety. The establishment of pool laws benefits servicers because they are often hired to help owners meet and keep up with safety regulations. A growing awareness among pool owners about the need to keep pools and hot tubs clean to prevent infection will continue to keep servicers in business.

Technological developments will also create more work for servicers. The need to maintain and repair new equipment, such as solar heaters, automatic timers, pool covers, and chemical dispensers, will keep pool services in demand.

For More Information

To read about issues affecting the swimming pool industry, visit the Aqua Magazine *Web page, or contact:*

Aqua Magazine
4130 Lien Road
Madison, WI 53704
Tel: 800-722-8764
Web: http://www.aquamagazine.com

To learn about scholarship opportunities, contact:

Independent Pool and Spa Service Association
17715 Chatsworth Street, Suite 203
Granada Hills, CA 91344
Tel: 888-360-9505
Web: http://www.ipssa.com

For information on education and certification programs, contact the following organizations:

National Spa and Pool Institute
2111 Eisenhower Avenue
Alexandria, VA 22314
Tel: 703-838-0083
Web: http://www.nspi-austin.com

National Swimming Pool Foundation
PO Box 495
Merrick, NY 11566
Tel: 516-623-3447
Web: http://www.nspf.com

Tailors and Dressmakers

Art Family and consumer science Mathematics	School Subjects
Artistic Following instructions	Personal Skills
Primarily indoors Primarily one location	Work Environment
High school diploma	Minimum Education Level
$15,870 to $18,630 to $32,290	Salary Range
None available	Certification or Licensing
Decline	Outlook

Overview

Tailors and dressmakers cut, sew, mend, and alter clothing. Typically, tailors work only with menswear, such as suits, jackets, and coats, while dressmakers work with women's clothing, including dresses, blouses, suits, evening wear, wedding and bridesmaids' gowns, and sportswear. Tailors and dressmakers are employed in dressmaking and custom tailor shops, department stores, and garment factories; others are self-employed. Approximately 74,000 custom tailors work in the United States.

History

The practice of making and wearing clothing evolved from the need for warmth and protection from injury. For example, in prehistoric times, people wrapped themselves in the warm skins of animals they killed for food. Throughout history, the making of clothing has been practiced by both men and women, in all cultures and every economic and social class.

Early clothing styles developed according to the climate of the geographical area: skirts and loose blouses of thin fabrics in warmer climates, pants and coats of heavier fabrics in cold climates. Religious customs and occupations also affected clothing styles. But as civilizations grew more and more advanced, clothing as necessity evolved into clothing as fashion.

The invention of the spinning wheel, in use in the 12th century, sped the process of making threads and yarns. With the invention of the two-bar loom, fabric making increased, styles became more detailed, and clothing became more widely available. Fabric production further increased with other inventions, such as the spinning jenny that could spin more than one thread at a time, power looms that ran on steam, and the cotton gin. The invention of the sewing machine tremendously sped the production of garments, although tailors and dressmakers were never completely replaced by machines.

During the Industrial Revolution, factories replaced craft shops. High-production apparel companies employed hundreds of workers. Employees worked 12- to 14-hour workdays for a low hourly pay in crowded rooms with poor ventilation and lighting. The poor working conditions of these factories, known as "sweatshops," led to the founding of The International Ladies Garment Workers Union in 1900 and the Amalgamated Clothing Workers of America in 1914; these unions protected workers' rights, ensured their safety, and led to greatly improved working conditions.

Today, the precise skills of tailors and dressmakers are still in demand at factories, stores, and small shops. The limited investment required to cut and sew garments, the wide availability of fabrics, and the demand for one-of-a-kind, tailor-made garments are factors which continue to provide opportunities for self-employed tailors and dressmakers.

The Job

Some tailors and dressmakers make garments from start to completion. In larger shops, however, each employee usually works on a specific task, such as measuring, patternmaking, cutting, fitting, or stitching. One worker, for example, may only sew in sleeves or pad lapels. Smaller shops may only measure and fit the garment, then send piecework to outside contractors. Some tailors and dressmakers specialize in one type of garment, such as suits or wedding gowns. Many also do alterations on factory-made clothing.

Tailors and dressmakers may run their own businesses, work in small shops, or work in custom tailoring sections of large department stores. Some work out of their homes. Retail clothing stores, specialty stores, bridal shops, and dry cleaners also employ tailors and dressmakers to do alterations.

Tailors and dressmakers first help customers choose the garment style and fabric, using their knowledge of the various types of fabrics. They take the customer's measurements, such as height, shoulder width, arm length, and waist, and note any special figure problems. They may use ready-made paper patterns or make one of their own. The patterns are then placed on the fabric and the fabric pieces are carefully cut. When the garment design is complex, or if there are special fitting problems, the tailor or dressmaker may cut the pattern from inexpensive muslin and fit it to the customer; any adjustments are then marked and transferred to the paper pattern before it is used to cut the actual garment fabric. The pieces are basted together first and then sewn by hand or machine. After one or two fittings, which confirm that the garment fits the customer properly, the tailor or dressmaker finishes the garment with hems, buttons, trim, and a final pressing.

Some tailors or dressmakers specialize in a certain aspect of the garment-making process. *Bushelers* work in factories to repair flaws and correct imperfect sewing in finished garments. *Shop tailors* have a detailed knowledge of special tailoring tasks. They use shears or a knife to trim and shape the edges of garments before sewing, attach shoulder pads, and sew linings in coats. *Skilled tailors* put fine stitching on lapels and pockets, make buttonholes, and sew on trim.

Requirements

High School

While in high school, you should get as much experience as you can by taking any sewing, tailoring, and clothing classes offered by vocational or home economics departments. There are also a number of institutions that offer either on-site or home study courses in sewing and dressmaking. Art classes in sketching and design are also helpful. Math classes, such as algebra and geometry, will help you hone your ability to work with numbers and to visualize shapes.

Postsecondary Training

Tailors and dressmakers must have at least a high school education, although employers prefer college graduates with advanced training in sewing, tailoring, draping, patternmaking, and design. A limited number of schools and colleges in the United States offer this type of training, including Philadelphia University, the Fashion Institute of Technology in New York City, and the Parsons School of Design, also in New York. Students who are interested in furthering their career, and perhaps expanding from tailoring into design, may want to consider studying in one of these specialized institutions. It is, however, entirely possible to enter this field without a college degree.

Other Requirements

Workers in this field must obviously have the ability to sew very well, both by hand and machine, follow directions, and measure accurately. In addition to these skills, tailors and dressmakers must have a good eye for color and style. They need to know how to communicate with and satisfy customers. Strong interpersonal skills will help tailors and dressmakers get and keep clients.

Exploring

Take sewing classes at school. Also, check with your local park district or fabric and craft stores—they often offer lessons year-round. Find summer or part-time employment at a local tailor shop. This will give you valuable work experience. Contact schools regarding their programs in Fashion Design. If their course descriptions sound interesting, take a class or two. You can also create and sew your own designs or offer your mending and alteration services to your family and friends. Finally, visit department stores, clothing specialty stores, and tailor's shops to observe workers involved in this field.

Employers

Those interested in high fashion should check out haute couture houses such as Chanel or Yves Saint Laurent. These industry giants deal with expensive fabrics and innovative designs. They also cater to a high level of clientele. Be prepared for stiff competition because such businesses will only consider the most experienced, highly skilled tailors and dressmakers.

Tailors and dressmakers employed at retail department stores make alterations on ready-to-wear clothing sold on the premises. They may perform a small task such as hemming pants or suit sleeves, or a major project such as custom fitting a wedding dress.

In some cases, it is possible for tailors or dressmakers to start their own businesses by making clothes and taking orders from those who like their work. Capital needed to start such a venture is minimum since the most important equipment, such as a sewing machine, iron and ironing board, scissors, and notions, are widely available and relatively inexpensive. Unless the tailor or dressmaker plans to operate a home-based business, however, he or she will need to rent shop space. Careful planning is needed to prepare for a self-owned tailoring or dressmaking business. Anyone running a business needs to learn bookkeeping, accounting, and how to keep and order supplies. A knowledge of marketing is important too, since the owner of a business must know how, when, and where to advertise in order to attract customers. Tailors or dressmakers planning to start their own businesses should check with their library or local government to learn what requirements, such as permits, apply. Finally, don't forget to consult established tailors and dressmakers to learn the tricks of the trade.

Starting Out

Custom tailor shops or garment manufacturing centers sometimes offer apprenticeships to students or recent graduates, which gives them a start in the business. As a beginner you may also find work in related jobs, such as a sewer or alterer in a custom tailoring or dressmaking shop, garment factory, dry cleaning store, or department store. Apply directly to such companies and shops and monitor local newspaper ads for openings, as well. Check with your high school's career center to see if they have any industry information or leads for part-time jobs. Trade schools and colleges that have programs in textiles or fashion often offer their students help with job placement.

Advancement

Workers in this field usually start by performing simple tasks. As they gain more experience and their skills improve, they may be assigned to more difficult and complicated tasks. However, advancement in the industry is typically somewhat limited. In factories, a production worker might be promoted to the position of line supervisor. Tailors and dressmakers can move to better shops that offer higher pay or open their own businesses.

Some workers may find that they have an eye for color and style and an aptitude for design. With further training at an appropriate college, these workers may find a successful career in fashion design and merchandising.

Earnings

Salaries for tailors and dressmakers vary widely, depending on experience, skill, and location. According to the 1998 Apparel Plant Wages Survey, conducted by the American Apparel Manufacturers Association, the average hourly earnings were about $7.63, which made for an annual salary of roughly $15,870. Experienced workers in supervisory sewing positions earned a weekly average of $477. Cutting room supervisors earned a weekly average of about $621. These weekly earnings made for an annual income of approximately $32,290. The median annual salary for custom tailors reported by the U.S. Department of Labor in 1998 was $18,630.

Workers employed by large companies and retail stores receive benefits such as paid holidays and vacations, health insurance, and pension plans. They are often affiliated with one of the two labor unions of the industry—the International Ladies Garment Workers Union and the Amalgamated Clothing and Textile Workers of America—which may offer additional benefits. Self-employed tailors and dressmakers and small-shop workers usually provide their own benefits.

Work Environment

Tailors and dressmakers in large shops work 40 to 48 hours a week, sometimes including Saturdays. Union members usually work 35 to 40 hours a week. Those who run their own businesses often work longer hours. Spring and fall are usually the busiest times.

Since tailoring and dressmaking require a minimal investment, some tailors and dressmakers work out of their homes. Those who work in the larger apparel plants may find the conditions less pleasant. The noise of the machinery can be nerve-wracking, the dye from the fabric may be irritating to the eyes and the skin, and some factories are old and not well maintained.

Much of the work is done sitting down, in one location, and may include fine detail work that can be time consuming. The work may be tiring and tedious and occasionally can cause eye strain. In some cases, tailors and dressmakers deal directly with customers, who may be either pleasant to interact with, or difficult and demanding.

This type of work, however, can be very satisfying to people who enjoy using their hands and skills to create something. It can be gratifying to complete a project properly, and many workers in this field take great pride in their workmanship.

Outlook

According to the U.S. Department of Labor, employment prospects in this industry are expected to decline through 2008. Factors attributing to the decline include the low cost and ready availability of factory-made clothing and the invention of labor saving machinery such as computerized sewing and cutting machines. In fact, automated machines are expected to replace many sewing jobs in the next decade. In addition, the apparel industry has declined domestically as many businesses choose to produce their items abroad where labor is cheap and, many times, unregulated.

Tailors and dressmakers who do reliable and skillful work, particularly in the areas of mending and alterations, however, should be able to find employment. This industry is large, employing thousands of people. Many job openings will be created as current employees leave the work force due to retirement or other reasons.

For More Information

For information on careers in the apparel manufacturing industry, contact:

American Apparel and Footwear Association
1601 North Kent Street, Suite 1200
Arlington, VA 22209
Tel: 800-520-2262
Web: http://www.americanapparel.org

For a listing of home study institutions offering sewing and dressmaking courses, contact:

Distance Education and Training Council
1601 18th Street, NW
Washington, DC 20009-2529
Tel: 202-234-5100
Email: detc@detc.org
Web: http://www.detc.org

For information packets on college classes in garment design and sewing, contact the following schools:

Fashion Institute of Design and Merchandising
919 South Grand Avenue
Los Angeles, CA 90015
Tel: 800-711-7175
Web: http://www.fidm.com

Fashion Institute of Technology
Seventh Avenue at 27th Street
New York, NY 10001-5992
Tel: 212-217-7999
Email: FITinfo@fitsuny.edu
Web: http://www.fitnyc.suny.edu/

Parsons School of Design
66 Fifth Avenue
New York, NY 10011
Tel: 800-252-0852
Web: http://www.parsons.edu

Tax Preparers

Business Mathematics	School Subjects
Following instructions Helping/teaching	Personal Skills
Primarily indoors Primarily one location	Work Environment
Some postsecondary training	Minimum Education Level
$19,500 to $27,510 to $39,050	Salary Range
Required by certain states	Certification or Licensing
About as fast as the average	Outlook

Overview

Tax preparers prepare income tax returns for individuals and small businesses for a fee, either for quarterly or yearly filings. They help to establish and maintain business records to expedite tax preparations and may advise clients on how to save money on their tax payments. There are approximately 79,000 tax preparers employed in the United States.

History

President Franklin D. Roosevelt (1882-1945) once said, "Taxes are the dues that we pay for the privileges of membership in an organized society." Although most people grumble about paying income taxes and filling out tax forms, everyone carries a share of the burden, and it is still possible to keep a sense of humor about income taxes. As Benjamin Franklin (1706-90) succinctly said, "In this world nothing can be said to be certain, except death and taxes."

While the personal income tax may be the most familiar type of taxation, it is actually a relatively recent method for raising revenue. To raise funds for the Napoleonic Wars between 1799 and 1816, Britain became the first nation to collect income taxes, but a permanent income tax was not established there until 1874. In the same manner, the United States first initiated a temporary income tax during the Civil War. It wasn't until 1913, however, with the adoption of the 16th Amendment to the Constitution, that a tax on personal income became the law of the nation. In addition to the federal income tax, many states and cities have adopted income tax laws. Income taxes are an example of a "progressive tax," one that charges higher percentages of income as people earn more money.

Technology has now made it possible to file taxes electronically. Electronic tax filing is a method by which a tax return is converted to computer readable form and sent via modem to the Internal Revenue Service. Electronically filed tax returns are more accurate than paper filed returns because of the extensive checking performed by the electronic filing software. Detecting and correcting errors early also allows the tax return to flow smoothly through the IRS, speeding up the refund process. New computer software is also available which gives individuals a framework in which to prepare and file their own taxes.

The Job

Tax preparers help individuals and small businesses keep the proper records to determine their legally required tax and file the proper forms. They must be well acquainted with federal, state, and local tax laws, and use their knowledge and skills to help taxpayers take the maximum number of legally allowable deductions.

The first step in preparing tax forms is to collect all the data and documents that are needed to calculate the client's tax liability. The client has to submit documents such as tax returns from previous years, wage and income statements, records of other sources of income, statements of interest and dividends earned, records of expenses, property tax records, and so on. The tax preparer then interviews the client to obtain further information that may have a bearing on the amount of taxes owed. If the client is an individual taxpayer, the tax preparer will ask about any important investments, extra expenses that may be deductible, contributions to charity, and insurance payments; events such as marriage, childbirth, and new employment are also important considerations. If the client is a business, the tax preparer may ask about capital gains and losses, taxes already paid, payroll expenses, miscellaneous business expenses, and tax credits.

Once the tax preparer has a complete picture of the client's income and expenses, the proper tax forms and schedules needed to file the tax return can be determined. While some taxpayers have very complex finances that take a long time to document and calculate, others have typical, straightforward returns that take less time. Often the tax preparer can calculate the amount a taxpayer owes, fill out the proper forms, and prepare the complete return in a single interview. When the tax return is more complicated, the tax preparer may have to collect all the data during the interview and perform the calculations later. If a client's taxes are unusual or very complex, the tax preparer may have to consult tax law handbooks and bulletins.

Computers are the main tools used to figure and prepare tax returns. The tax preparer inputs the data onto a spreadsheet, and the computer calculates and prints out the tax form. Computer software can be very versatile and may even print up data summary sheets that can serve as checklists and references for the next tax filing.

Tax preparers often have another tax expert or preparer check their work, especially if they work for a tax service firm. The second tax preparer will check to make sure the allowances and deductions taken were proper and that no others were overlooked. They also make certain that the tax laws are interpreted properly and that calculations are correct. It is very important that a tax preparer's work is accurate and error-free, and clients are given a guarantee covering additional taxes or fines if their work is found to be incorrect. Tax preparers are required by law to sign every return they complete for a client, along with providing their Social Security number or federal identification number. They must also provide the client with a copy of the tax return and keep a copy in their own files.

Requirements

High School

Although there are no specific postsecondary educational requirements for tax preparers, you should certainly get your high school diploma. While you are in high school there are a number of classes you can take that will help prepare you for this type of work. Naturally, take mathematics classes. Accounting, bookkeeping, and business classes will also give you a feel for working with numbers and show you the necessity for accurate work. In addition, take computer classes. You will need to be comfortable using computers since much tax work is done using this tool. Finally, take English classes. English classes will help you work on your research, writing, and speaking skills—important communication skills to have when you work with clients.

Postsecondary Training

Once you have completed high school, you may be able to find a job as a tax preparer at a large tax preparing firm. These firms, such as H & R Block, typically require their tax preparers to complete a training program in tax preparation. If you would like to pursue a college education, many universities offer individual courses and complete majors in the area of taxation. Another route is to earn a bachelor's degree or master's degree in business administration with a minor or concentration in taxation. A few universities offer master's degrees in taxation.

In addition to formal education, tax preparers must continue their professional education. Both federal and state tax laws are revised every year, and the tax preparer is obligated to understand these new laws thoroughly by January 1 of each year. Major tax reform legislation can increase this amount of study even further. One federal reform tax bill can take up thousands of pages, and this can mean up to 60 hours of extra study in a single month to fully understand all the intricacies and implications of the new laws. To help tax preparers keep up with new developments, the National Association of Tax Practitioners offers more than 200 workshops every year. Tax service firms also offer classes explaining tax preparation to both professionals and individual taxpayers.

Certification or Licensing

Licensing requirements for tax preparers vary by the state, and you should be sure to find out what requirements there are in the state where you wish to practice. Since 1983, for example, tax preparers in California have been required to register with the state Department of Consumers. Tax preparers who apply for registration in that state must be at least eighteen years old and have a high school diploma or the equivalent. In addition, they need to have 60 hours of formal, approved instruction in basic income tax law, theory, and practice, or two years of professional experience in preparing personal income tax returns.

The Internal Revenue Service offers an examination for tax preparers. Those who complete the test successfully are called *enrolled agents* and are entitled to legally represent any taxpayer in any type of audit before the IRS or state tax boards. (Those with five years' experience working for the IRS as an auditor or in a higher position can become enrolled agents without taking the exam.) The four-part test is offered annually and takes two days to complete. There are no education or experience requirements for taking the examination, but the questions are roughly equivalent to those asked in a college course. Study materials and applications may be obtained from local IRS offices. The IRS does not oversee seasonal tax preparers, but local IRS offices may monitor some commercial tax offices.

To be eligible to process returns and transmit them directly to the Internal Revenue Service via modem, tax preparers must apply to the IRS to become an Electronic Return Originator. A background check and fingerprinting may be required.

The Institute of Tax Consultants offers an annual open book exam to obtain the title of Certified Tax Preparer. Certification also requires 30 hours of continuing education each year.

Other Requirements

Tax preparers should have an aptitude for math and an eye for detail. They should have strong organizational skills and the patience to sift through documents and financial statements. The ability to communicate effectively with clients is also key to be able to explain complex tax procedures and to make customers feel confident and comfortable. Tax preparers also need to work well under the stress and pressure of deadlines. They must also be honest, discreet, and trustworthy in dealing with the financial and business affairs of their clients.

Exploring

If a career in tax preparation sounds interesting, you should first gain some experience by completing income tax returns for yourself and for your family and friends. These returns should be double-checked by the actual taxpayers who will be liable for any fees and extra taxes if the return is prepared incorrectly. You can also look for internships or part-time jobs in tax service offices and tax preparation firms. Many of these firms operate nationwide, and extra office help might be needed as tax deadlines approach and work becomes hectic. The IRS also trains people to answer tax questions for its 800-number telephone advisory service; they are employed annually during early spring.

Try also to familiarize yourself with the tax preparation software available on the Internet and utilize Web sites to keep abreast of changing laws, regulations, and developments in the industry. The National Association of Tax Practitioners offers sample articles from its publication, *Tax Practitioners Journal,* online. (See end of article for contact information.)

Employers

Tax preparers may work for tax service firms such as H & R Block and other similar companies that conduct most of their business during tax season. Other tax preparers may be self-employed and work full- or part-time.

Starting Out

Because tax work is very seasonal, most tax firms begin hiring tax preparers in December for the upcoming tax season. Some tax service firms will hire tax preparers from among the graduates of their own training courses. Private and state employment agencies may also have information and job listings as will classified newspaper ads. You should also consult your school guidance offices to establish contacts in the field.

There are a large number of Internet sites for this industry, many of which offer job postings. Many large tax preparation firms, such as H & R Block, also have their own Web pages.

Advancement

Some tax preparers may wish to continue their academic education and work toward becoming certified public accountants. Others may want to specialize in certain areas of taxation, such as real estate, corporate, or nonprofit work. Tax preparers who specialize in certain fields are able to charge higher fees for their services.

Establishing a private consulting business is also an option. Potential proprietors should consult with other self-employed practitioners to gain advice on how to start a private practice. Several Internet sites also give valuable advice on establishing a tax business.

Earnings

According to the *O*Net Dictionary of Occupational Titles,* the yearly income for tax preparers was approximately $19,500. The Economic Research Institute reported that in 1999 the average starting annual salary for tax preparers was $27,510. Those with 10 years of experience reported an average yearly income of approximately $39,050. Incomes can vary widely from these figures, however, due to a number of factors. One reason is that tax preparers generally charge a fee per tax return, which may range from $30 to $1,500 or more, depending on the complexity of the return and the preparation time required. Therefore, the number of clients a preparer has as well as the difficulty of the returns can affect the preparer's income. Another factor affecting income is the amount of education a tax preparer has. Seasonal or part-time employees, typically those with less education, usually earn minimum wage plus commission. Enrolled agents, certified public accountants, and other professional preparers, typically those with college degrees or more, usually charge more. Finally, it is important to realize that fees vary widely in different parts of the country. Tax preparers in large cities and in the western United States generally charge more, as do those who offer year-round financial advice and services.

Work Environment

Tax preparers generally work in office settings which may be located in neighborhood business districts, shopping malls, or other high traffic areas. Employees of tax service firms may work at storefront desks or in cubicles during the three months preceding the April 15 tax-filing deadline. In addition, many tax preparers work at home to earn extra money while they hold a full-time job.

The hours and schedules that tax preparers work vary greatly, depending on the time of year and the manner in which they are employed. Because of the changes in tax laws that occur every year, tax preparers often advise their clients throughout the year about possible ways to reduce their tax obligations. The first quarter of the year is the busiest time, and even part-time tax preparers may find themselves working very long hours. Workweeks can range from as little as 12 hours to 40 or 50 or more, as tax preparers work late into the evening and on weekends. Tax service firms are usually open seven days a week and 12 hours a day during the first three months of the year. The work is demanding, requiring heavy concentration and long hours sitting at a desk and working on a computer.

Outlook

The U.S. Department of Labor predicts that employment for tax preparers will grow as fast as the average for all other occupations through 2008. According to the IRS, 53 percent of U.S. taxpayers prepare their own returns, but because tax laws are constantly changing and growing more complex, demand for tax professionals will remain high. Much of this demand, however, is expected to be met by the tax preparers already working because computers are increasingly expediting the process of tabulating and storing data. Recent surveys of employers in large metropolitan areas have found an adequate supply of tax preparers; prospects for employment may be better in smaller cities or rural areas.

Although tax laws are constantly evolving and people look to tax preparers to save time, money, and frustration, new tax programs and online resources are easing the process of preparing taxes, lessening the need for outside help. Information is available at the touch of a button on tax laws and regulations. Tax tips are readily available as are online seminars and workshops.

The IRS currently offers taxpayers and businesses the option to "e-file," or electronically file their tax returns on the Internet. While some people may choose to do their own electronic filing, the majority of taxpayers will still rely on tax preparers—licensed by the IRS as Electronic Return Originators—to handle their returns.

For More Information

For information on the Certified Tax Preparer designation, contact:

Institute of Tax Consultants
7500 212th SW, Suite 205
Edmonds, WA 98026
Tel: 425-774-3521
Web: http://taxprofessionals.homestead.com/welcome.html

For industry information, contact:

National Association of Tax Consultants
PO Box 90276
Portland, OR 97290-0276
Tel: 800-745-6282
Web: http://www.natctax.org

For information on educational programs, publications, and online membership, contact:

National Association of Tax Practitioners
720 Association Drive
Appleton, WI 54914-1483
Tel: 800-558-3402
Email: natp@natptax.com
Web: http://www.natptax.com/

For training programs, contact:

H & R Block
Web: http://www.hrblock.com

For information on becoming an enrolled agent or an Electronic Return Originator, check out the IRS Web site:

Internal Revenue Service
Department of Treasury
Web: http://www.irs.ustreas.gov

Taxi Drivers

Business Mathematics	School Subjects
Following instructions Helping/teaching	Personal Skills
Primarily indoors Primarily multiple locations	Work Environment
High school diploma	Minimum Education Level
$11,544 to $15,558 to $25,875+	Salary Range
Required by all states	Certification or Licensing
About as fast as the average	Outlook

Overview

Taxi drivers, also known as *cab drivers,* operate automobiles and other motor vehicles to take passengers from one place to another for a fee. This fee is usually based on distance traveled or time as recorded on a taximeter. There are currently over 100,000 taxi drivers in the United States.

History

Today's taxis are the modern equivalent of vehicles for hire that were first introduced in England in the early 1600s. These vehicles were hackneys, four-wheeled carriages drawn by two horses that could carry up to six passengers. By 1654, there were already 300 privately owned hackneys licensed to operate in London. In the next century, hackneys were introduced in the United States. Around 1820, a smaller vehicle for hire, the cabriolet, became common in London. At first it had two wheels, with room only for a driver and one passenger, and one horse drew it. Some later cabriolets, or cabs, as they were soon called, were larger, and by mid-century, a two-passenger version, the hansom cab, became the most popular cab in London. Hansom cabs were successfully brought to New York and Boston in the 1870s.

Toward the end of the 19th century, motorized cabs began to appear in the streets of Europe and America. From then on, the development of cabs paralleled the development of the automobile. The earliest motorized cabs were powered by electricity, but cabs with internal combustion engines appeared by the early 20th century. Along with the introduction of these vehicles came the need for drivers, thus creating the cab driver profession. In 1891, a device called a "taximeter" (tax is from a Latin word meaning "charge") was invented to calculate the fare owed to the driver. Taximeters found their first use in the new horseless carriages for hire, which were soon called "taxicabs" or just "taxis."

The use of taxis has increased especially in metropolitan areas where there is dense traffic, increasing population, and parking limitations. Modern taxis are often four-door passenger cars that have been specially modified. Depending on local regulations, the vehicles may have such modifications as reinforced frames or extra heavy-duty shock absorbers. Taxi drivers may be employees of taxi companies, driving cars owned by the company; they may be lease drivers, operating cars leased from a taxi company for a regular fee; or they may be completely independent, driving cars that they own themselves.

The Job

Taxicabs are an important part of the mass transportation system in many cities, so drivers need to be familiar with as much of the local geographical area as possible. But taxicab drivers are often required to do more than simply drive people from one place to another. They also help people with their luggage. Sometimes they pick up and deliver packages. Some provide sightseeing tours for visitors to a community.

Taxi drivers who are employed by, or lease from, a cab service or garage report to the garage before their shift begins and are assigned a cab. They receive a tripsheet and record their name, date of work, and identification number. They also perform a quick cursory check of the interior and exterior of the car to ensure its proper working condition. They check fuel and oil levels, brakes, lights, and windshield wipers, reporting any problems to the dispatcher or company mechanic.

Taxi drivers locate passengers in three ways. Customers requiring transportation may call the cab company with the approximate time and place they wish to be picked up. The dispatcher uses a two-way radio system to notify the driver of this pick-up information. Other drivers pick up passengers at cab stands and taxi lines at airports, theaters, hotels, and railroad stations, and then return to the stand after they deliver the passengers. Drivers may pick up passengers while returning to their stands or stations. The third manner of pick up for taxi drivers is by cruising busy streets to service passengers who hail or "wave them down."

When a destination is reached, the taxi driver determines the fare and informs the rider of the cost. Fares consist of many parts. The drop charge is an automatic charge for use of the cab. Other parts of the fare are determined by the time and distance traveled. A taximeter is a machine that measures the fare as it accrues. It is turned on and off when the passenger enters and leaves the cab. Additional portions of the fare may include charges for luggage handling and additional occupants. Commonly, a passenger will offer the taxi driver a tip, which is based on the customer's opinion of the quality and efficiency of the ride and the courtesy of the driver. The taxi driver also may supply a receipt if the passenger requests it.

Taxi drivers are required to keep accurate records of their activities. They record the time and place where they picked up and delivered the passengers on a trip sheet. They also have to keep records on the amount of fares they collect.

There are taxis and taxi drivers in almost every town and city in the country, but most are in large metropolitan areas.

Requirements

High School

Taxi drivers do not usually need to meet any particular educational requirements, but a high school education will help you adequately handle the record-keeping part of the job. You should also take courses in driver education, business math, and English.

Certification or Licensing

In large cities, some taxi drivers belong to labor unions. The union to which most belong is the International Brotherhood of Teamsters, Chauffeurs, Warehousemen, and Helpers of America.

Those interested in becoming a taxi driver must have a regular driver's license. In most large cities, taxi drivers also must have a special taxicab operator's license—commonly called a hacker's license—in addition to a chauffeur's license. Police departments, safety departments, or public utilities commissions generally issue these special licenses. To secure the license, drivers must pass special examinations including questions on local geography, traffic regulations, accident reports, safe driving practices, and insurance regulations. Some companies help their job applicants prepare for these examinations by providing them with specially prepared booklets. The operator's license may need to be renewed annually. In some cities (New York, for example), new license applications can take several months to be processed because the applicant's background must be investigated. Increasingly, many cities and municipalities require a test on English usage. Those who do not pass must take a course in English sponsored by the municipality.

Other Requirements

If you plan on becoming a taxi driver you should be in reasonably good health and have a good driving record and no criminal record. In general, you must be 21 years of age or older to drive a taxicab. While driving is not physically strenuous, you will occasionally be asked to lift heavy packages or luggage. If you work in a big city, you should have especially steady nerves because you will spend considerable time driving in heavy traffic. You must also be courteous, patient, and able to get along with many different kinds of people.

Taxi drivers who own their own cab or lease one for a long period of time are generally expected to keep their cab clean. Large companies have workers who take care of this task for all the vehicles in the company fleet.

Exploring

Visit your local library to find books about taxi drivers and other transportation careers. Ask your teacher or guidance counselor to set up a talk with a taxi driver. Take a ride in a taxi to experience the career firsthand.

Employers

Taxi drivers are often employed by a cab service and drive cars owned by the company. Some drivers pay a fee and lease cabs owned by a taxi company while others own and operate their own cars. There are approximately 6,300 cab companies operating 171,000 taxicabs in the United States, according to the International Taxicab and Livery Association.

Starting Out

Usually people who want to be a taxi driver apply directly to taxicab companies that may be hiring new drivers. Taxicab companies are usually listed in the Yellow Pages. It may take some time to obtain the necessary license to drive a cab, and some companies or municipalities may require additional training, so it may not be possible to begin work immediately. People who have sufficient funds may buy their own cab, but they usually must secure a municipal permit to operate it.

Earnings

Earnings for taxi drivers vary widely, depending on the number of hours they work, the method by which they are paid, the season, the weather, and other factors. Median hourly earnings (excluding tips) for full-time taxi drivers were $7.48 in 1998, according to the U.S. Department of Labor. The lowest 10 percent of full-time taxi drivers earned $5.55 or less an hour, while the highest 10 percent averaged more than $12.44 an hour.

Limited information suggests that independent owner-drivers can average anywhere between $20,000 to $30,000 annually, including tips. This assumes they work the industry average of eight to ten hours a day, five days a week.

Many taxi drivers are paid a percentage of the fares they collect, often 40 to 50 percent of total fares. Other drivers receive a base amount plus a commission related to the amount of business they do. A few drivers are guaranteed minimum daily or weekly wages. Drivers who lease their cabs may keep all the fare money above the amount of the leasing fee they pay the cab company. Tips are also an important part of the earnings of taxi drivers. They can equal 15 to 20 percent or more of total fares. Most taxi drivers do not receive company-provided fringe benefits, such as pension plans.

Earnings fluctuate with the season and the weather. Winter is generally the busiest season, and snow and rain almost always produce a busy day. There is also a relationship between general economic conditions and the earnings of taxi drivers, because there is more competition for less business when the economy is in a slump.

Work Environment

Many taxi drivers put in long hours, working from eight to twelve hours a day, five or six days a week. They do not receive overtime pay. Other drivers are part-time workers. Drivers may work Sundays, holidays, or evening hours.

Taxi drivers must be able to get along with their passengers, including those who try their patience or expect too much. Some people urge drivers to go very fast, for example, but drivers who comply may risk accidents or arrest for speeding. Drivers may have to work under other difficult conditions, such as heavy traffic and bad weather. Taxi drivers must be able to drive safely under pressure. In some places, drivers must be wary because there is a considerable chance of being robbed.

Outlook

There will always be a need for taxi drivers. Job opportunities for taxi drivers are expected to grow about as fast as the average through 2008, according to the U.S. Department of Labor. The high turnover rate in this occupation means that many of the new job openings that develop in the future will come when drivers leave their jobs to go into another kind of work. In addition, as the American population increases and traffic becomes more congested, the need for taxi drivers will increase, especially in metropolitan areas. At present many drivers work on a part-time basis, and that situation is likely to continue.

For More Information

For additional information about the taxi driving profession, contact:

International Taxicab and Livery Association
3849 Farragut Avenue
Kensington, MD 20895
Tel: 301-946-5701
Web: http://www.taxinetwork.com/

Taxidermists

Art Biology Technical/shop	School Subjects
Artistic Mechanical/manipulative	Personal Skills
Primarily indoors Primarily one location	Work Environment
Some postsecondary training	Minimum Education Level
$15,000 to $30,000 to $50,000+	Salary Range
Required	Certification or Licensing
Faster than the average	Outlook

Overview

Taxidermists preserve and prepare animal skins and parts to create lifelike animal replicas. Taxidermists prepare the underpadding and mounting that the skin will be attached to, model the structure to resemble the animal's body, and then attach appropriate coverings, such as skin, fur, or feathers. They may add details, such as eyes or teeth, to make a more realistic representation. The animals they mount or stuff may be for private or public display. Museums frequently use creations from taxidermists to display rare, exotic, or extinct animals. Hunters also use taxidermists' services to mount fishing and hunting trophies for display. The National Taxidermists Association estimates there are about 75,000 taxidermists in the United States working full- or part-time.

History

Animal tanning and skin preservation has been practiced over the millennia for clothing, decoration, and weapons. Native Americans used tanned hides to make their lodgings. Trophies from hunts of dangerous animals were often worn to display the bravery of the hunter. Tanning methods included stringing skins up to dry, scraping them, and perhaps soaking them in water with tannins from leaves. Animal skins were preserved for many different purposes, but not specifically from interest in the natural sciences until the 18th century. Tanning methods improved during this time. Displaying the skin on models stuffed with hay or straw became popular for museums and private collections. Animals were posed realistically and backgrounds were added to the display areas in museums to show the habitat of the animal.

By the 19th century, taxidermy was a recognized discipline for museum workers. In Paris, Maison Verreaux became the chief supplier of exhibit animals. Carl Akeley, who worked for Ward's Natural Science Establishment in New York, mastered a taxidermic technique that allowed for realistic modeling of large animals such as bears, lions, and elephants. His works are still on display in the Chicago Field Museum of Natural History and the New York Natural History Museum. In recent years, several taxidermy supply companies have developed lifelike mannequins to be used as the foundation for fish, birds, and fur-bearing animals. Such new techniques in the art and science of taxidermy continue to be developed and used.

The Job

Taxidermists use a variety of methods to create realistic, lifelike models of birds and animals. Although specific processes and techniques vary, most taxidermists follow a series of basic steps.

First, they must remove the skin from the carcass of the animal with special knives, scissors, and pliers. The skin must be removed very carefully to preserve the natural state of the fur or feathers. Once the skin is removed, it is preserved with a special solution.

Some taxidermists still make the body foundation, or skeleton, of the animal. These foundations are made with a variety of materials, including clay, plaster, burlap, paper-mâché, wire mesh, and glue. Other taxidermists, however, use ready-made forms, which are available in various sizes so taxidermists simply take measurements of the specimen to be mounted and order the proper size from the supplier. Metal rods are often used to achieve the desired mount of the animal.

The taxidermist uses special adhesives or modeling clay to attach the skin to the foundation or form. Then artificial eyes, teeth, and tongues are attached. Sometimes taxidermists use special techniques, such as airbrushing color or sculpting the eyelids, nose, and lips. They may need to attach antlers, horns, or claws. Finally they groom and dress the fur or feathers with styling gel, if necessary, to enhance the final appearance of the specimen.

Taxidermists work with a variety of animal types, including one-cell organisms, large game animals, birds, fish, and reptiles. They even make models of extinct animal species, based on detailed drawings or paintings. The specific work often depends on the area of the country where the taxidermist is employed, since the types of animals hunted vary by region.

Requirements

High School

Successful taxidermy requires many skills. Workers must have good manual dexterity, an eye for detail, knowledge of animal anatomy, and training in the taxidermy processes. High school classes in art, woodworking, and metal shop may help develop the skills necessary for this career. Also, a class or classes in biology might be helpful in teaching the student the bodily workings of certain animals.

Postsecondary Training

In the United States, several schools offer programs or correspondence courses in taxidermy. Courses often last from four to six weeks, and subjects such as laws and legalities, bird mounting, fish mounting, deer, small mammals, diorama-making, air and brush painting, and form-making are covered. Taxidermists who hope to work in museums should expect to take further training and acquire additional skills in related subjects, which they can learn in museum classes.

Certification or Licensing

Taxidermists are required to be licensed in most states, with specific licensing requirements varying from state to state. Many taxidermists choose to become members of national or local professional associations. The largest of these, the National Taxidermists Association (NTA), offers the designation of Certified Taxidermist to members who have met specific requirements. Members may be certified in one or all four categories of specialization: mammals, fish, birds, and reptiles. Certification indicates that they have reached a certain level of expertise and may allow them to charge a higher price for their work.

Exploring

Because taxidermy is a specialized occupation, there are few opportunities for part-time or summer work for students, though some larger companies will hire apprentices to help with the work load. However, you may learn more by ordering video tapes and beginning mounting kits to experience the mounting process. Other good learning opportunities include speaking to a museum taxidermist or writing to schools or associations that offer courses in taxidermy. Check with the NTA for upcoming conventions and seminars which are open to the public. Time spent at such an event would not only provide a solid learning experience, but a chance to meet and mingle with the pros.

Employers

Taxidermists can be found throughout the United States and abroad. Experienced and established taxidermists, especially those with a large client base, will often hire apprentices, or less experienced taxidermists, to assist with larger projects or undertake smaller jobs. Contact the NTA for a listing of such employers.

The majority of taxidermists, about 70 to 80 percent, are self-employed, according to Greg Crain, executive director of the NTA. His advice to aspiring entrepreneurs? Hone your skills in business, as well as your craft. Accounting, advertising, and marketing are good background courses to help any small business owner. Be prepared to attend to the many details of running a business such as maintaining an inventory of chemicals and supplies, advertising and promotion, and pricing your work.

Starting Out

Taxidermy is a profession that requires experience. Most workers start out as hobbyists in their own homes, and eventually start doing taxidermy work part time professionally. Later, after they have built up a client base, they may enter the profession full time. Jobs in existing taxidermy shops or businesses are difficult to find, because most taxidermists are self-employed and prefer to do the work themselves. However, in some cases, it may be possible to become a journeyman or apprentice and work for an already established taxidermist on either an hourly basis or for a percentage of the selling price of the work they are doing.

Jobs in museums are often difficult to obtain: applicants should have a background in both taxidermy and general museum studies. Taxidermy schools primarily train their students to become self-employed but may sometimes offer job placement as well.

Advancement

Advancement opportunities are good for those with the proper skills, education, and experience. Taxidermists who can work on a wide range of projects will have the best chances of advancing. Since larger game animals bring more money, one method of advancing would be to learn the skills necessary to work on these animals. Taxidermists who develop a large customer base may open their own shop. Workers employed in museums may advance to positions with more responsibilities and higher pay.

Earnings

It is very difficult, if not impossible, to determine a nationwide earnings figure for taxidermists. The individual's level of experience, certification, speed, and quality of work are all factors that significantly affect income. Most taxidermists will charge by the inch or the weight of the animal. Difficult mounts, or unusual background accessories may add significantly to the final price. Here's an example: an open mouth on an animal, as opposed to a droopy mouth, or a closed mouth, can add about $100 to the price of a mounting. In addition, the region of the country and the type of game typically hunted and mounted are important variables. Most new taxidermists, however, might expect to earn about $15,000 annually. Those with 5 to 10 years of experience and a proven level of quality could earn $30,000 or more. Some exceptional taxidermists can earn upwards of $50,000 annually. Museum workers might also expect to average $20,000 yearly.

Because most are self-employed, or work for a very small operation, few taxidermists have any sort of benefits package. Those who work in museums may, however, be offered health insurance and paid vacation and sick leave.

Work Environment

Most taxidermists work 40 hours a week, although overtime is not uncommon during certain times of the year. Taxidermists with their own shops may have to work long hours, especially when first starting out. They must often work with strong-smelling chemicals and sharp tools, and possibly diseased animals. If working on smaller animals and birds, they can sit or stand. However, creating larger mammal displays may require more physical work, such as climbing or squatting.

Workers in taxidermy will find it satisfying to see a project from beginning to completion. There is also the element of pride in good craftsmanship; it can be gratifying for workers to use their talents to recreate extremely realistic and lifelike animal forms.

Outlook

The job outlook for taxidermists should be good over the next decade. Although jobs in museums may be scarce, the demand for hunting and fishing trophies continues to provide work for taxidermists. It is not unusual for qualified taxidermists to have a year's worth of work backlogged. In addition, many educational institutions actively seek models of animal and bird species that are nearing extinction. Talented taxidermists who can take on a variety of projects should be able to find steady employment. Those with an eye for unique poses and mounts, or unusual expressions will be in high demand.

For More Information

For information on the industry, certification, taxidermy schools, trade magazines, association membership, and career opportunities, contact:

National Taxidermists Association
108 Branch Drive
Slidell, LA 70461
Tel: 504-641-4682
Email: ntahq@aol.com
Web: http://www.taxidermy.net

For information on training in taxidermy, contact the following schools:

Missoula Valley School of Taxidermy
PO Box 1169
Thompson Falls, MT 59873
Tel: 406-827-3170
Web: http://www.nwmontana.com/mvst.htm

Northwood School of Taxidermy
116 Main Street
Stoystown, PA 15563
Tel: 814-893-5386
Web: http://northwoodtaxidermy.com/

Rinehart School of Taxidermy
3032 McCormick Drive
Janesville, WI 53545
Tel: 888-804-0773
Web: http://www.taxidermyonline.com/school.html

Southland School of Taxidermy
2603 Osceola Street
Baton Rouge, LA 70805
Tel: 225-356-2903
Web: http://www.taxidermyschool.com/

Index